Cats Do It Better Than People

200 Life Lessons You Can Learn from Your Feline Friend

Theresa Mancuso

Adams Media
Avon, Massachusetts

Published by
Adams Media, an F+W Publications Company
57 Littlefield Street, Avon, MA 02322. U.S.A.
www.adamsmedia.com

ISBN: 1-59337-281-7

Printed in Canada.

J I H G F E D C B A

Library of Congress Cataloging-in-Publication Data
Mancuso, Theresa.
Cats do it better than people / Theresa Mancuso.
p. cm.
ISBN 1-59337-281-7
1. Cats—Anecdotes. 2. Cats—Behavior—Anecdotes.
3. Human-animal relationships—Anecdotes. I. Title.
SF445.5.M34 2005
636.8'0887—dc22
2004026389

All interior photography provided by Theresa Mancuso. The photograph on page 21 was taken by Theresa Mancuso, but the cats belong to Fran Nickerson, owner of Spielzeit Tonkinese Cattery.

Dedication

For David Rodgers and Maruca

And in memory of John "Jack" Vinson,
also known as "Silver Coyote,"
a contributor to this anthology.
September 1, 1940–April 14, 2004

And for my wonderful feline family,
living and deceased:

Ludmilla
Jasmine
Maximus
Theodosius
Carlotta
Nikki
Primo
Marmaduke Rodgers
Charles Andrew Shen
Jack Daniels Goldstene
and
Honey Bear

Contents

Foreword

HAVE YOU EVER HAD A FELINE FRIEND with whom you shared an almost mystical bond? Everyone fortunate enough to have had that experience says there's nothing comparable to being owned by an adoring cat.

I was developing that rapport with my own special cat when I first met Theresa Mancuso nineteen years ago. She had just acquired Nikki, a Tonkinese kitten with whom she achieved a very special relationship. We visited together at cat shows, at her apartment in New York, and at my home in Wisconsin.

"Irrepressible" is the description that comes to mind to best describe Theresa. I knew her as a writer, photographer, former nun, who integrated her love of animals into everything that she did.

One doesn't need to think like a cat to fully understand why cats do what they do, but it helps. Theresa has put together a collection of tales from cat lovers throughout the world. The tales in this book may provide insight into questions you've had, but not known whom to ask. Enjoy!

—FRAN NICKERSON,
Owner of Spielzeit Tonkinese Cattery,
registered 1984, numerous regional and breed wins,
more than fifty CFA Grand Champion and Grand Premiers

Acknowledgments

I PURR IN ACKNOWLEDGMENT of everyone who contributed to this book, the anecdote authors, my wonderful literary agent, the inimitable Sara Camilli, and my superb project editor, Kate Epstein.

Grateful purrs also go to family and friends for their help and encouragement in bringing this project along. I especially thank my longtime friend and mentor, Mary Shen, for her endless proofreading of the manuscript and for continuing to assist me with all of my fur-kids, canine and feline. Generous purrs and gentle scratches of appreciation go to my sister Carolina and my brother-in-law David Rodgers for their never-failing help and support, and to Jack Ryan, my friend and supervisor at the New York City Department of Probation where I work, for all that he has taught me about the art of journalism and editing.

Purrful thanks to Fran Nickerson of Spielzeit Tonkinese Cattery for writing the Foreword.

Finally, with raucous purrs of appreciation, I acknowledge all the good people who feed and rescue feral cats, strays, and other homeless felines that wander about in search of food. These animal lovers daily feed the "poor" cats, not because they *have* to, but because they *want* to. They are nameless for the most part, but I know several by name and see them regularly on their missions of mercy. Thank you in the name of Kittydom, Al Wilson, Enid Coel, Edna Wak, Vera, Margie, Marion, Laura, Karen, Lorraine, Melie, and Diane. Most of all, with heartfelt appreciation for everything they have done, *not only for the cats*, but for me, I thankfully acknowledge Lois and Marjorie Goldstene and Judy Casey for extending my feline connections.

Introduction

CATS ARE AMONG the most beautiful creatures on earth. They fascinate us with their elegance, scintillating beauty of form, shape, color, texture, and movement. They capture our minds and hearts with their nobility and grandeur. What's not to love in a cat?

Cat watchers are everywhere! Our delight is in all things feline: cat photos, cat paintings, stuffed toys in the form of cats, cat calendars, cat-shaped pillows, and the real thing, of course, cats of every size and kind. Sometimes, their runaway cat fancy results in an overflow of cats living in a single household. Feline lovers understand this phenomenon for cats are irresistible. There are an amazing number of cat addicts out there. This book proves that fact, if nothing else. Many cultures held cats in awe and even worshipped felines for their majestic qualities and awesome intelligence. Cats have never forgotten this.

Cats have been real-life heroes, and, though (sad to say), they have often been maligned, portrayed unjustly as villains, those humans who share their lives with cats recognize how much they contribute. Yes, my friends, cats *do* teach us in marvelous ways. They are singularly untainted by corruption or deceit, beautiful and wise, intelligent and loyal. No wonder we love cats. What's not to love in such magnificent beings?

The sound of the cat mesmerizes, calms the chattering mind, stills the anxious heart. Watching cats helps us see the universe with different eyes. The anecdotes in this anthology are ordinary tales written by ordinary people with extraordinary love for cats. The stories illuminate how felines improve our lives. May this book inspire you to find the cat of your dreams, perhaps a stray or shelter feline desperately in need of someone to love. Maybe not just one, but several. There's a dream cat or two out there waiting just for you.

1

Cats Are for Lovin'

Romance and Friendship

Kittens and cats are cuddlers that gift us with the magnificent pleasure of touch. Hold a cat against your heart; take in positive health benefits, a truth supported by medical research. Cats ease blood pressure, soothe stress, and induce calm. They warm us with their soft fur and make us feel good. During life's great journey, love and friendship, romance and companionship are great gifts, and yes, cats have something to say about love. They seem to believe they perfected it! For cats—and for us, life is all about loving, the most important thing we'll ever do. The wisdom we may glean from feline friends will certainly improve the quality of romance and friendship in our lives. Go ahead, cuddle with your cat and it will teach you about all love and friendship. Primo, my cat, sits atop my computer nodding his approval! Cuddled up with Abby, my German shepherd dog, as close to my computer desk as they can get, are the other felines in our household, Marmaduke, Charlie, Jack Daniels, and Honey Bear. Welcome to the wonderful world of cats.

The Marshmallow Cat

by Sharon Ulrich

Years ago, I found myself at an animal shelter, struggling to decide which kitten to take. I watched one clumsily make its way to my outstretched hand. This fluffy ball of gray and white fur promptly bit my finger, and that was the life-altering day that Kazmurak entered my heart.

I was a floundering university student, confused and uncertain about which direction to take. Like many other students, I existed on junk food, but I always fed my cats the best. My two older felines were content with their expensive all-natural diets, but not Kazmurak. He was my constant companion during mealtimes, but I was convinced I knew what was best, so human food was off limits.

That was until the fateful marshmallow day when I came home from class and was greeted at the door by a marshmallow. I followed the half-eaten marshmallow trail that led me onto shelves, under blankets, into the bathroom, and finally to an overstuffed gray and white belly attached to an extremely satisfied cat.

At that moment I found my vocation: I decided to obtain a degree in animal behavior, and now I'm a feline behaviorist. I learned that there are hidden messages in the things creatures do; we just have to learn to interpret their meanings.

As for Kazmurak, he never did eat another marshmallow, but there's always the "hotdog bun incident". . .

You never know what will show you the way to your life's work.

Dancing with My Cat

by Anna Haltrecht

Bamboo, soft and orange, walks across the polished floor, pauses, listens, and waits. He likes the music that is playing. I crawl steadily towards him, attempting to be as catlike as he. He kneads the floor, lifting each paw high into the air and purposely placing it down. I copy him.

He lightly steps in a circle around me. I turn to face him as he stops and we mirror each other in kneading. Suddenly, he plops down and rolls luxuriously from side to side; again, I copy his movements, our heads leading us each in our own arc. We are dancing together, rolling around, stepping, walking, crawling, and then a jump. How joyful! When he tires, Bamboo leaps gracefully onto the table and falls asleep.

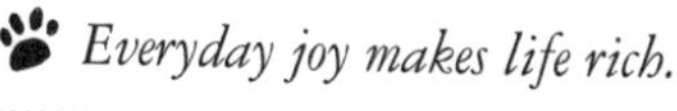
Everyday joy makes life rich.

Best Friends

by Rebecca Eitemiller (12 years old)

I have a cat named Snickers. He is really a sweetheart! Whenever I get mad, Snickers is always there to cheer me up and never gets annoyed in return. Snickers is truly one of my best friends. Some time ago, before I got Snickers, our family had a very lovable kitty named Boots. When I would get out of the shower and go to bed to read, Boots would be waiting for me on my pillow, ready to nibble my hair. Maybe most people wouldn't like this very much, but it was the only way I could get her to purr me to sleep, so I didn't mind. I loved to hear her purr.

One night we let Boots out and she never came back. There are coyotes in this part of the country, so when Boots did not return after a couple of months, I assumed that the coyotes got her. It was really hard to get over it, but after a year or so, I felt ready to get a new cat. Mom said I could and we got Snickers. Since then, Snickers and I have been the best of friends. I still think of Boots often, but Snickers always makes me smile!

The best healing after the loss of a beloved pet is to obtain a new pet. Not that one would ever replace the other, but when you give your nurturing love to a new individual, your grief will be more quickly healed.

Go Away!

by Rod Marsden

Kathy didn't want a cat. However, a tough little tortoise-colored tom had other ideas. He followed her home from school.

"Go away!" she cried, but he just cocked his head and looked up at her with his one green eye and his one hazel eye. When she started walking, he started walking, too.

Her mother said that if she didn't feed him he'd soon go away. The very next day, the unfed cat was back.

"Your cat's got funny eyes," Ginny, a school friend, told her, "but you could do worse."

"Maybe this cat is different," ventured her mother that evening. "Maybe we need to feed it to get rid of it." They gave it boneless chicken scraps and nondairy cat milk they got from a neighbor who had an old Siamese.

The cat was happy and followed Kathy to school and back with a new spring in its stride. The next morning, her mother not only found the cat on her porch but a dead mouse as well.

"I don't think he'll be going in a hurry," her mother said. "We could take him to the RSPCA where he'd probably last three weeks before they put him to sleep."

"Oh no!" cried Kathy. "We can't let that happen . . . to Scruff."

"We'll have to clean him up and feed him every day."

"Well!" pouted Kathy. "If he's going to follow me around, he better be the best damned cat he can be!"

Be open to love when it comes.

Pepi Ringtail

by Barbara H. Vinson

Bet you've never seen a ring-tailed cat. I don't mean tabby rings, I mean a natural white ring two-thirds of the way down a black tail. That's Pepi Ringtail! One day, my friend Alice called me saying that she had just brought home a new kitten from Hoboken. Would I like to come over and meet him?

When I arrived at Alice's and she showed me that lil' old black-and-white ring-tailed character, I was totally smitten. I said to Alice, "All I can say is, it's a good thing you saw him before I did!" I really meant that; I was so envious! A few days later, Alice called and told me that she was unable to keep Pepi after all, so if I wanted him, I could have him. I nearly dropped the phone. Did I want Pepi? Was I dreaming? I could scarcely believe my good fortune!

That was ten years ago, and Pepi's been an absolute joy for every single one of them. He has an unusually sweet, mellow disposition. He's one of those that Molly, our little matriarch, washes the most frequently. One of his most endearing traits is to sit and look at you, head cocked to one side and one paw raised. When he pulls that one, you just want to eat him up!

Pepi is super special, no doubt about it, one of those rare souls that when they made him, they broke the mold.

When you give true love, it will be rewarded.

My Furry Family Loves *The New York Times*

by Theresa Mancuso

My neighbors are avid readers of *The New York Times.* I never buy the newspaper, but my commitment to it has grown over the years, and now no one could appreciate it more. Its versatility is invigorating. Every Tuesday, I search the recycling area in our coop for the Sunday *Times.* I gather them up and take them home, where carefully, I check through every page, reading items "fit to print" that provide me with insight and appreciation for my world, albeit two days late.

I open several pages at a time and lay them on the floor, making a goodly cushion in a hidden corner of my apartment. The *Times* is there for my German shepherd, who, at six years of age and spayed, sometimes has bathroom needs while I am away at work or asleep during the night. Before Abby has her go at the superabsorbent pages, and even while they are being spread, my cats enjoy a favorite pastime: running wildly beneath the pages of the *Times,* they create mountains of moving print.

In the evening after work, I find Abby's canine lake in the center of the pile and now the cats are nowhere near it. Already dry, these pages are ready for another use. I lift them and hasten to the cat box where I scoop out used litter and wrap it in the newspaper, rolling it up and securing it in used grocery bags. Then, as mysteriously as it arrived, bundle disappears down the trash chute, having served us well. That's why my furry family loves *The New York Times*.

Willful waste brings woeful want; recycle and safeguard the earth.

A Wise and Faithful Friend

by Mary Shen

The kitten was a stray in the courtyard on Grand Street when Tanya took it home. Cinnamon was a grown cat by the time Tanya's son, Anthony, was born and was always a loving presence in their home. She considered herself, no doubt, to be the couple's first (furry) daughter, and Anthony, their first son. A dark domestic shorthair, Cinnamon was remarkably intelligent. She bonded with infant Anthony. Should he cry, she was first at his crib to see what was the matter. When Anthony began to creep, Cinnamon stayed nearby, moving the tip of her tail to attract his attention. The baby would reach out and grab it. Cinnamon sat beside him on the couch while he played with his toys, and as Anthony grew into boyhood, she was his devoted companion. She stood guard while he slept and sprawled out comfortably on the couch beside him when he read. When he came home from school, Cinnamon sniffed Anthony thoroughly, rubbing up against his legs, checking him out by walking all around him.

He was a rambunctious kid, but he never mistreated his cat. When Anthony was thirteen and Cinnamon was eighteen, everybody noticed that he was growing taller and taller, and sadly, they also noticed that dear old Cinnamon was growing thinner and thinner, until she slipped away into her final rest. A little boy's perfect friend was gone but not forgotten!

Quiet vigilance and loving presence are the expression of perfect, trustful love.

From "Get Away!" to "Mine, Mine, MINE!"

by Lisa Sanders

Whoever said that feral cats cannot be tamed and turned into "love bugs" was really wrong. After being out from six in the evening until four in the morning one day in May, with both my hands torn to shreds from failed attempts to catch a feral cat, I was about to give up on the little guy in my backyard, who could have been a twin brother to my female kitten inside.

She was Feline Leukemia positive (FeLV+) and taking in another cat worried me, but still, I felt I just had to catch him and find out if they were related. They looked so much alike with their rare spotted coats. The next day, I set a trap, and within an hour I had him. I brought him into the house and let him sit quietly in the cage for some time to calm down.

It seemed that we made very little progress during the first week. I was frantic trying to find someone to give him a vet check and neuter him. You could spend all day in the bathroom where he was confined, and he would just ignore you and mind his own business, playing, eating, and using his litter box. If you tried to touch him or showed any interest, off he went into hiding.

Then, one day, out of the blue, he ran past me while I was sitting with him. I reached out to scratch his back. He stopped, turned around, crept back to me with his tail twitching, and sat down to look me over. I reached out again and scratched his head. This time, he leaned forward and sniffed my hand. Then, he rubbed all he could into my hand. I could hardly believe it! My feral friend was purring. Then, he charged off and hid himself again. The same thing happened the next day and the next. Finally, he leaped up into my lap, curled himself in a tiny ball, and purred contentedly.

Now, Indy (short for Indiana Jones, because of his fearless personality and his prowess as a true lady's man—or cat) purrs constantly and is a healthy, happy, vaccinated cat, FeLV-free and devoted to his twin sister, the FeLV+ kitten who looks just like him.

Taking a chance on love and friendship is worth the risk.

The Irresistible Magic of Marmaduke Rodgers

by Theresa Mancuso

I drove my friend to the local shelter to adopt a puppy. My friend went off to look at available pups, and I went into the feline adoptables' room, where I was drawn immediately to a corner cage in which a tiny red tabby was climbing the walls. The kitten looked at me with complete confidence as I opened the cage and took him out. He must have been experienced with people, for without a moment's hesitation, he climbed to my shoulder and pressed his tiny face to my cheek. Wise kitty that he was, he snuggled close while his motor idled, purring. The magic of his tiny voice as he chirped—not a meow but a true chirp—was a most delicious sound, and soon it made me melt.

I take my people as they come, but I usually like my animals purebred. Was I to adopt a shelter cat? The question loomed large.

While I was struggling to assess the implications of an affirmative response, the little red tiger lifted a soft paw to caress my face. It was magic and forever! Off we went to the processing counter to begin the adoption process. The next day, neutered and micro-chipped, Marmaduke Rodgers came to his forever home. As elegant as a purebred show cat, he walked confidently up to Primo, my British shorthair, and this alley-born boy from the sidewalks of east New York introduced himself with a proffered paw.

Be open to the possibilities of love and friendship wherever, whenever you meet them.

....

Toby

by Barbara H. Vinson

Toby is a very dark tortoiseshell cat—black with little spots of orange here and there, so that she reminds you of the night sky in October. She has a "star" on top of her head and wears a "necklace" of stars.

In Manhattan, Toby lost her original home by smacking her owner's landlady (she must have deserved it) and was put back up for adoption. One day, Judy and Patty asked me if I'd foster Toby for a week or so, to which I agreed. On the following Saturday, "adoption day," Judy came and waited in her car while I went to get Toby. When Toby spotted her carrier, she put two and two together and bolted. You know those fights and skirmishes in the funny papers where you see a big puff of dust with arms and legs sticking out of it? Well, that's what trying to capture Toby was like. She fought tooth and nail, she hissed, she growled, she spit, she scratched, she roared—I could not get that cat into her carrier. In the end, Judy had to leave without her.

One week later, the scenario repeated itself and we gave up. But eventually, we got her to "agree" to come with us.

That was a good five years ago. Toby is now living with us in Minnesota, and no doubt about it, she's deliriously happy with the home *she* has chosen. Toby is an easygoing cat, but when she says no, *no* is what she means.

There are times when you just have to put your foot down to make the "right thing" happen.

Misapprehension

by Lyn McConchie

One early afternoon on a very overcast day, I was crocheting an almost completed blanket when Tiger created minor confusion. An acquaintance from the village dropped in to talk about something and after several minutes eyed me uncertainly.

"Are you OK?" she asked.

I'm crippled, but I didn't think I looked worse off than usual. I wondered briefly why she would think I was not well, and I reassured her that I was. The conversation went on a bit longer, but then as she turned to go, she paused and looked me over. Then, she took a step closer and spoke.

"Are you sure you're OK? It sounds as if you have indigestion or something. I know you are given a lot of things, like painkillers and stuff. You'd say if you weren't well, wouldn't you?"

Inside me a sudden huge grin spread from ear to ear. I suppressed it valiantly while turning back the edge of the blanket I was crocheting: there, in my lap, comfortably curled asleep under the weight of woolly crocheting, was Tiger, giving his occasional soft growling snores.

My visitor gulped and hastily showed herself out, leaving me free to collapse in wails of laughter, to Tiger's surprise. He sat up, looked around, saw nothing, and went back to sleep.

Maybe he thought, *Humans are strange at times. They laugh for no reason.*

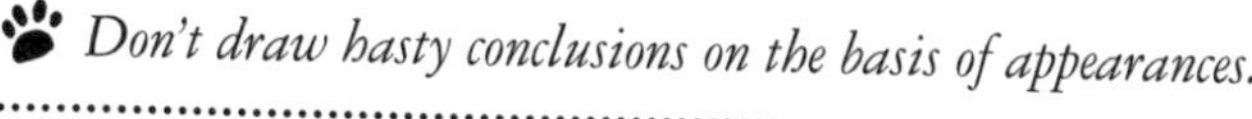

Don't draw hasty conclusions on the basis of appearances.

Give Your Heart a Break

by Theresa Mancuso

After living in a religious community for more than twenty years, my inner compass took a turn of its own, and I began the process of creating a new life, a journey that proved to me the powerful impact animals have on human well-being.

Ludmilla was a tiny gray tabby I adopted from a newspaper ad. Splendidly kittenish, Ludi's vigorous motor mouth never ceased uttering gracious purrs, a healing sound that soothed my heart as I pined for the monastic life I had left behind. Ludmilla had all the makings of a forever cat, as did Jasmine, who came along several months later.

When I rented my first apartment, I took delight in selecting new furniture, but soon I realized the damage thirty-two sharp claws could inflict on the fabric of a new couch and chairs. In one of the most regretted moves I have ever made (in a lifetime sufficiently full of them!) I surrendered my purring partners to a member of my parish who promised to turn them over to her sister for a new home in the country. I've regretted my abandonment of Ludi and Jasmine for the last twenty-two years.

Their purrs and tender kitty caresses more than deserved the fidelity of a forever home with me, but alas, I had not yet formed my convictions about animals. All I could think of was the beauty of my furnishings being destroyed. Ludi and Jasmine had restored peace to my heart when I needed their comforting presence. Jasmine, I learned, took over the farm, but Ludi died of a broken heart.

Never abandon a friend. Do what you must to go forward with your life, but never, ever be unfaithful in love or friendship.

Sometimes Love Is Not Enough

by Theresa Mancuso

Who wouldn't love Carlotta? Named for the famous ballerina of the nineteenth century, Carlotta Grisi (little Lotti) possessed her own coquettish appeal, and not a bad voice, either—reminiscent of the great court dancer and opera singer. Lotti was a platinum Tonkinese showgirl. Though she was just a local yokel from the Bronx, she wanted to be a great lady of world renown just as her namesake was.

Whiskers to tail, Lotti was a razzle-dazzle cat. I felt lucky when her breeder decided to retire her from show business. Giving Lotti to me was an act of pure friendship, but alas, sometimes love is just not enough. Although I loved Carlotta, it didn't take more than a brief introductory period to realize that Lotti didn't love my other cats. Forget about it, she positively hated them. What to do?

Lotti made an about-face and returned to her original mom. A while later, to everyone's relief, Carlotta became the only cat in an adoring household somewhere in Arizona. Far from the dizzying shows and her almost-siblings in Brooklyn, Lotti basks in everlasting glory with her purrfect new mom.

Sometimes love is not enough and other courses must be pursued. Be brave and true to yourself in facing up to reality.

Sunrise

by Catherine Miller

Our eyes met across a crowded room . . . This much is true, but the romance was all on my side of the experience. It was a crowded exhibition hall. Through the thin bars of his show cage, I was the last image he saw as his eyelids grew heavier and finally succumbed to the seduction of an afternoon snooze. Winning all those ribbons was, after all, hard work.

Since then, I have become Sunrise's housekeeper and slave. The vacuuming never seems to end. When I get home from work, he leads me immediately to the litter box for cleaning, and vocalizes his displeasure until it is spotless. Next it's off to the dry food dish, where he meows until the slightly stale food is removed and fresher morsels are added. After these duties are completed, it is time for grooming. I comb him and wash the tear stains off his face, and he reciprocates by combing my long hair with his tongue and rubbing his cheeks against my hand and face to make me smell just like him.

He is right to scold me in his gentle way, of course. If only I would give up my day job and stay home with him, he wouldn't need to wait for things to be put right! Then we could cuddle all day and take naps together. The fur and feathers would fly as Sunrise frolicked around the house, chasing his feathers-on-a-stick and soccer balls around, pouncing and kicking them to a much-loved pulp . . . not to mention the movies we would bliss out watching together—fish and bird extravaganzas, such as *Finding Nemo* and *Winged Migration*.

Great love and devotion are always a blessing to the giver.

Dilemma

by Caroline McRae-Madigan

When I was a young girl, we always had cats. I was about eight when we got yet another kitten and I was finally going to name my first cat. Dilemma—that should have been the cat's name. As time wore on, no one could tell if this was a boy or girl—a very important fact to an eight-year-old trying to find the perfect name for her new pet. Finally, I could wait no more. I announced to everyone that if it were a boy, his name would be Charlie, and if it were a girl, then Anne. (I had just finished reading *Anne of Green Gables*!) Everyone was to call my cat Charlie-Anne.

His name stuck with him for life. Charlie-Anne was my best friend through my teenage years. He slept with me and purred me to sleep every night, even after I married. Charlie-Anne was the one who prepared me for parenthood, and he was even with me when my son was born. It was not long after that when Charlie-Anne said goodbye, without ever being sick a day in his life, without ever causing me a moment's worry. I awoke one morning to find him not on my pillow, but under my baby's crib where he had passed on.

Friendship means understanding, compassion, companionship, generosity, and many other qualities that serve the needs of the ones we love.

Contributor's Note: I want to dedicate this story to my father, Jim McRae of Chetwynd, Ontario, who passed away last year. One of my fondest memories is of watching him stand on a chair and hold one of our cats up to the ceiling so he could catch a fly.

My Boy

by Carol Osborne

Years ago, I had a cat who was just all "mine." He tolerated others, but he was my special friend. When I left town for any length of time, he would get in my bed under the covers and not come out (except to eat late at night) while I was away.

The strange thing was that about thirty minutes before I returned home, that cat buddy of mine would materialize and prance around like he was a happy boy. How he knew that I was on my way back home, no one ever figured out, but he never failed to appear thirty minutes before I arrived home after a trip! Sadly, this great telepathic boy passed away at a ripe old age, but I still continue to look for him every time I come back home.

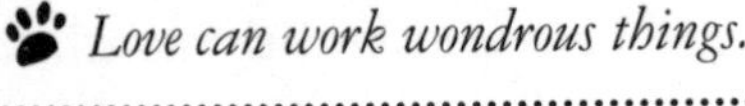
Love can work wondrous things.

Kitty Offspring

by Anne Fawcett

After I eloped, the first question I was asked by almost everyone was, "Are you pregnant?"—as if reproduction were the inevitable and most desirable consequence of tying the knot.

I usually explained that, no, I'm not the maternal type. Offspring were unlikely to appear in the near future. "Human offspring," I qualified. Today, my friends point out that my maternal instincts do exist—it's just that our two cats are the beneficiaries. In their minds, Mike and Lil' Puss are poor substitutes for something more substantial.

"That will change," they threaten, "when your biological clock starts ticking."

The assumption that I am training for motherhood on a lesser species before graduating to *Homo sapiens* does not stand up to scrutiny. My cats are not children but adults. While they rely on me for food and shelter, they are not dependent on me for all of their bodily functions. I'm happy to let them wander, and vice versa. We appreciate our differences and accept our limitations.

Human infants are constantly changing and developing. We have language, sensation, and thought in common with them. There is no comparison.

My friends and I agree that cats can never be adequate substitutes for human family. But I argue that cats don't need this role as "child substitute" to justify their place in our lives. It would, after all, be a very lonely planet if we could only share our lives with our own species.

March to your own drummer and heed your own inner light.

2

Purrfect Cat Communities

Virtues for Family Life

Cats are often thought to be loners, but in fact, they may live quite harmoniously in feline communities. They negotiate their lives quite well with others, and in doing so, they teach us to live better among our associates, especially in the closeness of family life. It takes some effort to introduce a new cat into the group. In my experience, the newcomer is always accepted sooner or later, and life goes on. But it is not always such a smooth transition—just as things can be a little rough for humans transitioning into a new community, so it goes for cats. Do we not all have obstacles to overcome in pursuit of peace and order? Cats often do it better than people!

Calamity's Battle

by P.M. Griffin

Two tiny pregnant felines lounged in the warm, spring sun. Provisions were plentiful and the yard was peaceful. Pauline called the gray tabby Missy. She named the other cat Calamity Jane because of her endless, though harmless, misfortunes. Missy and Calamity Jane shared the responsibilities of motherhood, feeding, grooming, and comforting their four kittens. Because duties were alternated, the babies were never alone for more than a few seconds.

The situation seemed idyllic until a huge devil tomcat appeared in the neighborhood. Word was that nineteen kittens had perished beneath his fangs. One day, screams and snarls rang out, followed by the deep growls of felines preparing for combat. Pauline's breath froze in her throat as she watched. The enormous tomcat crouched in attack posture before the nesting box, howling a battle call. Missy lay within, hissing and snarling, her body covering the helpless kittens. Unquestionably, she would fight, but to what purpose? Not much bigger than a half-grown kitten herself, she would be shredded as easily as the babies she guarded.

Moving almost too fast for the eye to follow, a small form flung itself between the combatants. It was Calamity Jane, ears flat against her head, eyes like slits! Her lips were drawn back in a snarl. Scarcely pausing to collect herself after her charge, she sprang at the tom. The first swipe of his paw slammed her against the wall.

Before he could resume his attack, she was back. The killer struck her aside. Again, Calamity returned. Then, the odds of war changed. Pauline arrived, broom in hand, screaming like a harpy. The devil tom exploded to half again his size as every hair stood erect. He yowled in terror and streaked from the yard before the broom had done more than thud solidly on the ground behind him.

Missy remained in her box, watching Pauline through round eyes. A bump against Pauline's calf caused her to glance down: Calamity was rubbing her face against Pauline's leg, purring her appreciation and approval. They had all done their part. Their tentative bond was now solid. Two- and four-legged, they were family.

Nothing forges stronger bonds than sticking together against a common threat.

....

My "Grandcat" and Me

by Rose Hosp

Marilyn, my "grandcat," has lived in four states, so far: Nevada, Arizona, Tennessee, and Utah. While her owners were living in Tennessee, she got to visit us in central New York State for Christmas. Being accustomed to checking out new places, Marilyn immediately and methodically inspected each room upon her arrival. When inspection was over, it appeared we had passed. It didn't take her long to claim several spots she deemed comfortable, including the windowsill directly behind the Christmas tree. No, she never disturbed an ornament! She readily settled into her new routine in the new surroundings.

Having never shared my home with an indoor pet and being one to startle easily, I knew I was in for an interesting week. Even so, Marilyn and I frightened each other only a couple of times. I'd jump when she'd appear out of nowhere; this, in turn, would startle her and off she'd run. The worst fright was at the computer. I was hacking away when she came in and sat next to my chair seemingly to observe, and so I continued with the computer. Suddenly, she jumped into my lap—as was her custom at home—scaring the wits out of me. This, of course, scared the wits out of her and off she raced. Had my son warned me that she was prone to do this, I might have remained more calm . . . *might* have.

Learning to live together is an important lesson for humans and felines alike.

All My Kitties

by Karen Heist

My son was born in 1996 and, like me, he loves cats. Being a small child, though, he gets too rough with them sometimes. Our cat, Sam, likes to gnaw on human toes—including my son's, so I had to tell him, "If you don't have shoes on, watch out!" I explained that Sam didn't mean any harm but was only being affectionate.

Suidia was by far the best cat I ever had. Suidia lived to be almost seventeen years old before being diagnosed with a tumor on her kidney. It was heartbreaking to put her to sleep. Always a happy cat, Suidia was much loved and is greatly missed. Now we have three cats, and Little Sammy has taken charge.

At the SPCA, I got a cat that my son named Jesse. Jesse is three years old and has a broken tail. He's cross-eyed and nervous, but we love him to death because he's so sweet. The other cats took to him in about three weeks.

Then we were offered a two-year-old cat named Maizy. It took poor Maizy three months to feel comfortable in her new home. We dubbed her "Crazy Maizy" because she doesn't seem happy unless she bites my mother every morning.

Sammy is "top cat," always provoking a fight, while Maizy plays along. Shane, the dog, must feel like he's going bonkers trying to keep track of all those felines.

There's always room for one more in a happy home.

Tracking Cat

by Theresa Mancuso

Abby lies on the old Ikea rug doing a long-down-stay as commanded, not a muscle twitching, good dog that she is. I hurriedly go through the apartment stashing away little food piles for her breakfast, hiding them in reachable, but out-of-the way places. When finished, I release her from the long-down-stay, saying, "Go find!" and Abby flies through the apartment, nose down as she tracks her breakfast, one pile at a time, with the best treats saved for last.

Now, anyone who knows cats readily understands that there's no such thing as a long-down-stay, or any other type of obedience command that a self-respecting cat will entertain, let alone perfectly obey. Cats do their own thing, not yours. But Abby is a dog and so she loves this game. It gives her a job to do, as well as a good breakfast, when I leave for the office every morning.

Often as not, a bewildered Abby looks up at me as she approaches her stash. (I do not leave until I see the first few discoveries!) Right beside her, or a little in front, tracking on his own terms (which means long before I give the "Go find" command), Charlie is gobbling down kibble and other morning fare. Forget that he has already eaten a hearty feline breakfast. Charlie leaps delightfully from one hiding place to the next, wolfing down whatever morsels he can grab before Abby catches up with him. They are often nose-to-nose on the food pile, eighty-six pounds of German shepherd and nine pounds of alley-cat kitten.

And so they continue every day: Abby faithfully executes a correct tracking routine, while Charlie stalks and pounces utilizing the feline approach.

Blessed are those able to earn their daily bread and share it with the ones they love.

....

Gangster Turned Nursemaid

by Theresa Mancuso

Early one blustery, rainy morning after Thanksgiving, I was walking my German shepherd dog when I spied a tiny white and black creature, barely visible in the shadows, but clearly walking toward us. I tied Abby to the fence and proceeded alone.

The kitten turned and scooted along the other side of the fence, where I was able to reach over and scoop him up into my arms.

Evidently not a feral cat, perhaps he was a pitiful baby throw-away. Who knows? He seemed to belong in my arms, cuddled under my coat. Later, my neighbor told me she had seen him wandering about the night before. I couldn't abandon him, and the next day, the weather turned absolutely horrible. He would surely have perished. So, I brought him to the vet the next day. Between a houseguest and myself, we named the waif Charles Andrew, held him, fed him, caressed him, talked to him, and introduced him gently to all the family pets.

My red cat, Marmaduke, had been a veritable gangster since we adopted him a year earlier. Overnight, he turned into the most devoted big brother I have ever met. He took care of Charlie in every way a cat boy can help another. Locked in Marmaduke's powerful cat arms, Charlie sleeps contentedly. What a miracle love can be. You never know when it's coming!

Never presume that character is a fixed unmovable thing. With proper motivation, anyone can improve.

Every Cat Counts

by Mary Rodgers Easton

Down in Abilene, we had a big red tabby named Tom that appeared in our backyard one day with a look that said, "Hey folks, I belong here." Up until then, I had many female rescues, but no males. Tom was our first male and also the first to discover that my mother liked to have heat on her back. Tom's vocation emerged when my mother lay down on the couch to rest, and he stretched himself out on her, applying his warm, furry body against her aching back. He was a purring, vibrating heating pad and the perfect masseur.

In our house, every cat counts, whether it's one with a mission, like Tom, or drop-in strays that stay forever, like the girls, Cleopatra, Lily Rose, Smudge, and Julie. Cleopatra is eight years old and her half-sister Lily Rose, known as Ms. Lily, is seven. Smudge (whose name means "little fire" in firemen's lingo) and Julie, our youngest, have their own cat tales. When I adopted Lily Rose, she was too young to leave her mother and never quite got over it. She still chews on things like telephone cords and other kitty delectables. Little Cleopatra was my companion for a short trip after Mother celebrated her one-hundredth birthday in 1995. Cleo rode in my arms and helped me write letters.

I'm not one to pay much attention to how I feel, but when I slipped and fell on the floor one day, all the cats gathered around, chirping away with concern. They wouldn't move, but settled nearby until help came. I needed bed rest to recover; they kept vigil there, too. Their attention made me realize how poorly I felt. Each one has a job to do, and every cat counts.

In a perfect family or community, everyone shares in the work, as well as the pleasure and play.

How Chip Saved Christmas

by Kimberly McDowell

When I saw the shaggy orphaned kitten at the local shelter, my heart melted. My daughter said, "Mom, it's almost Christmas. Let me get her for you."

After we had already processed the adoption and started off for home, my husband said, "We have too many pets already. I thought we agreed only on a male. I won't accept her and Chip won't like her. You should take her back." There was a stony silence in the car the rest of the way home. I cradled the kitten in my arms.

Chip, our eleven-month-old snowshoe Siamese absolutely adored the nine-week-old ball of fur that I named Christmas Fancy. When our other cat growled and hissed, my husband, vindicated, ignored the situation completely. But Chip was Fancy's staunch defender. He curled up with her on the couch and they slept. When Chip awakened, I picked him up and hugged him. "Chip," I said, "Mommy is proud of you. You made our new kitten welcome and that made Christmas happy for me."

Several minutes later, my husband lay down on the couch for his afternoon nap and picked up Fancy, cuddling her in the crook of his arm. They both fell asleep. We had a very wonderful Christmas thanks to Chip, whose loving and accepting spirit said more to my husband than a thousand words.

The best way to expel tension or hard feelings is by example, not words. Gentle, tender affection is never wasted, especially in the family, where we might forget how to relieve stress by kindness and affection.

Bedfellow from the Alley

by Theresa Mancuso

If any one had ever told me I'd become a cat lady, I'd have denied it vociferously! The very possibility of ever owning a single feline, let alone several, was a foreign thought to me. I was a dog person. Nevertheless, as the years go on, I can understand why many people become the sheltering arms for one species over another. Cats and other strays seem to understand when they have been rescued from their awful fate and given a second chance for happiness, or a third, or more.

Finding Charlie was nothing I had bargained for. Marmaduke was enough to keep me busy—trouble sufficient for any day. But Charlie was cold and small and lost on that windy November morning, and there was nothing to do but scoop him up and love him. And I did. Now it's payback time.

For keeping him warm and well fed, with his litter box cleaned and freshened at regular intervals, at least twice if not thrice a day or more, Charlie has thrived in his unexpected home. What is the return on this investment? Not a night passes that my bedfellow is not the most adoring, loving alley cat: Charles Andrew. He cannot sleep unless he has one paw touching me, a tiny kitten hand on my arm or shoulder. What reward could be better than my bedfellow from the alley?

Tenderness and touch deepen feelings of love and friendship.

The Dough Boys

by Patricia Clements

Among my animals are chickens rescued from battery farms that I feed bread and corn to daily. Others enjoy bread, too. The goats are partial, the pig catches crusts, and the donkey and pony hang around to snatch their share. The dogs wriggle through the wire to compete with the ducks and chickens, grabbing fallen morsels first, then trying to pluck up the courage to challenge the geese. What of the cats, you ask?

In the evening I leave the cats and dogs until last so they can enjoy the late sunshine. If it rains, they dash to the mobile home and racket around until bedtime.

At the rustle of plastic, everyone bleats, oinks, brays, meows, or barks *Bread!*—from sheep to goats to pigs to donkey to pony to cats and dogs—and I am obliged to dance around tearing slices into portions and distributing them. Occasionally, a cat has gone missing and turns up lurking in one of the chicken runs, trying desperately to disguise himself as a chicken in order to get more than his share.

Less charitable folks might suspect I am not feeding my animals enough, but my bank statement should convince them otherwise. How can I explain to two stunning Persian cats that bread is not their prescribed diet? My life would be simpler if they waited in line with the other felines for tins to be opened rather than tormenting me (not to mention scratching and clawing) for a portion of boring-looking bread!

There's no disputing taste, the ancients said. To each his own.

Kitten Rescues His Beloved Human

by Diana "Sue" Snyder

Although I probably was never really endangered, my kitten believes he rescued me. For various health problems, I find relief by sitting in the bathtub for a spell, the hotter the water, the better. Unfortunately, if I get too hot, I get dizzy. Occasionally, I've even passed out. Thus, when soaking, someone usually checks on me.

I leave the bathroom door ajar for cooler air and to let my cats and kittens come in. They love the water, and many of them climb into the tub or play nearby. Once, I was in the bathroom for a long time with the door closed. Someone was vehemently scratching the door. I figured the cats thought I was taking a bath and they were missing out, so I didn't respond.

Later on, although weak, I drew a bath, opened the door for air, and climbed into the tub. I slumped over the edge face down, resting my head on my arm. I must have dozed. I hadn't noticed the kitten coming in, but suddenly, I felt him trying to push my head up. Perched on the tub's edge with the top of his head pinned against mine, he was pushing with all his might. He kept on pushing until I gained the strength to raise my head. "Well, hello there," I said, and he began to purr and rub his face against my cheek. Success! I didn't drown. What a happy kitty!

It never hurts to check that someone you love is OK.

A New Forever Friend

by Theresa Mancuso

My grandniece Olivia was only fifteen months old when she made it clear to her devoted mom that she wanted a cat of her own. They visited a local shelter where her mom sought a gentle, unflappable cat that could accept the toddler's antics without hissing, scratching, or jumping up on her. The cat would be Olivia's first live-in animal companion, her first four-legged sibling, and it had to be just right for her.

The Cat Fairy Godmother must have overseen their quest, for immediately, there appeared a shiny black cat with large green eyes. His name was Rodger, but soon he would be called "Rodger Dodger" in hopes that he would learn to dodge Olivia when she stepped on him or pulled his ear. It didn't work. Mom observed attentively as Rodger entered Olivia's presence and cat and child met for the first time. Although Olivia uttered a ferocious and excited screech, Rodger Dodger just rubbed up against her legs quite calmly. Would he be gentle? Would he be kind? To Mom's delight and Olivia's boundless joy, it was love at first sight. The black cat continued to rub against her legs, purring his greeting. Olivia put her arms around him, laughing with delight. Rodger Dodger soon became Olivia's bosom buddy. They romp and play with abandon, and Rodger Dodger has a new forever home with Olivia.

Caring for a toddler requires great patience and love.

Why Cats Are Better Than People

by Glenda Moore

Cats don't care if you're gay or straight, what your religion is, or whether you're conservative or liberal. They don't care if you're a few pounds overweight. Cats aren't threatened if you earn more than they do. Cats don't have problems expressing affection in public, and if you piss 'em off, they walk away.

Cats don't dump you for another human. They don't need the latest designer fashions, and they don't care what you wear. Cats don't mind if you wear the same T-shirt and shorts for days on end. Cats don't drink beer and pass out on the floor. Cats don't blow smoke in your face or read at the dinner table. Cats don't brag about whom they've slept with or what they've done. Cats never correct your stories or interrupt you. They won't complain if you don't make the bed or do the dusting. Cats don't care if you leave the toilet seat up. Cats don't try to smooch you before you brush your teeth. They don't criticize your friends, and they're not threatened by your intelligence. You never have to wonder if a cat is lying. Cats don't make a practice of killing their own species. Cats don't mind if you do all the driving. They never step on the imaginary brake or holler, "Look out!" Cats (almost) always hit the litter box, and they're in and out in a hurry. You don't have to worry that your cat might do drugs or join a gang. And, last but not least, they don't ever try to take permanent possession of the remote control.

Things in ourselves, when found in others, often cause us annoyance and chagrin. Self-acceptance is the beginning of true charity toward others.

The Nagging Cat

by Jackie S. Brooks

Sammy Jo can be a bit of a nag; she sits on my desk with that disapproving look on her face every time I sit down to work at the computer. I can tell by the way she turns her back on me that she is thinking, *Here we go again. Can't she let that wretched machine alone for five minutes? When is she going to pay me the attention I deserve?* If I stay on the computer too long, she plonks herself down in front of the monitor or hangs over the keyboard, and if that doesn't work, she starts nagging in a very insistent voice.

Trouble is, she is "the boss"—the matriarch of our cat family. She keeps the younger cats in line, and she knows how to twist us around that soft velvet paw of hers. She can come in and go out of the cat-flap at will, but if one of us is around, she expects the door to be opened for her instead. Sammy Jo has plenty of curiosity, too. She inspects my cup and wrinkles her nose at the smell of my tea. She inspects my sandwich (just in case it's tuna). When I chop onions (*Oh boy, meat goes with onions!*), she soon comes running. If I receive a parcel, Sammy Jo helps to unwrap it. Most of all, she loves to be in the garden when I am there. Even though she is sixteen going on seventeen, she's still a kitten at heart and loves to play.

If you love someone, you can put up with some character flaws.

The Ice Cream Cat

by Theresa Mancuso

Charles Andrew Shen took to his new home with gusto, and soon adopted all the vices of the pack, the most obvious of which is our family's inordinate love for ice cream. There's no use denying that our pack gets high on ice cream, not every night, but often enough—too often to admit. Eating ice cream is our favorite overindulgence. Along came Charlie and we met our match. Enter the conquering hero of Ice Cream–aholics Not Anonymous.

The first time a pint of Carvel appeared on our dining room table after Charlie joined the pack, he vaulted from floor to tabletop in the blink of an eye and eagerly applied his tiny tongue to canvassing the surface of the open container, ingesting a steady flow of ice cream that disappeared into his tiny mouth with awesome speed. Nor did I (in the spirit of good discipline and training) attempt to stop him. From then on, there was no chance of ice cream in any disguise passing safely through his domain. Charlie launches like a rocket to stake his claim on every ice cream container in sight, even cones in the hand. Small comfort to those of us who suffer from the need to satisfy an ice cream addiction. Charles eats a goodly portion of ice cream before we even begin. His meows and his actions proclaim there's no shame to craving it, because he knows, as do we, that nothing tastes better than slightly melted ice cream.

Self-discipline is not easy for anyone.

All Modern Conveniences

by Louise Maguire

New Year's Eve: I had just snuggled into the feathery depth of the duvet when the window swung open.

"Chagall! I wish you'd learn to *shut* windows, too!" I yelled. The sleek cat sprang to my bed, tinkling mysteriously. Each black hair was a tiny icicle. Grumbling, I stepped over the dog, a sleepy boxer named Tabou, and shut the window. Chagall had cunningly occupied the hollow in my pillow and was engrossed in washing.

"Move over, you wretch." Chagall eased himself under my chin where he thawed and throbbed. He didn't demand breakfast at his usual hideously early hour but stayed buried under my duvet. A semisheathed paw dabbed me when I absentmindedly shoved a bare foot into his cozy corner.

The next day, my bedroom felt cooler than normal. "I wish you'd learn to shut windows, Chagall," I began, then remembered the window wasn't open. Apprehensively, I inspected our ever-reliable Swiss furnace. It was out. And it refused to fire—on New Year's Day, too! No tradesmen available. A housekeeper's nightmare.

Fortunately, with the oven on full blast, I could still heat the kitchen. I brought in the delicate plants and moved all the animals into the kitchen, and it felt just like being home in Scotland. Chagall wisely decided to retreat under the cooker, expected his meals there, and for once declined to share my bedroom. The only casualty was one tropical plant that died from cold.

There's no place like home.

The Virtues of Family Life

by Theresa Mancuso

People always ask if cats and dogs can really get along together. In our pack, it works like this. Every new addition is acquired as a youngster, which makes it easier for oldsters to accept. Introducing newcomers to older pets requires a bit of skill, a sense of humor, kindness and compassion, and determination that this family shall live together in peace, so help us God.

Primo, a chunky twelve-week-old British shorthair, had just flown in from Colorado. I took him from his carrier and held him in my arms while I relaxed and talked softly to my German shepherds, Grippi, Geisty, and Abby, and to Nikki, my Tonkinese, who was grieving her recently deceased Siamese companion. I let them draw near as they showed inclination to do so. Soon they were nose-to-nose and nose-to-butt, sniffing and licking the fearless, friendly Primo.

Years later, Nikki, Grippi, and Geisty passed away, leaving only Abby and Primo. I needed a buddy for Primo while Abby and I were out doing dog things. Enter Marmaduke. I introduced the squirming, climbing Marmaduke to Primo and Abby the same way I had introduced Primo. And so again with Charlie. They eat together, play together, and sleep together.

To my delight, I often see a pile of love around me, Charlie snuggled between Abby and me, and Marmaduke with his sleepy head on Abby's flank.

The key to living well together is mutual acceptance.

Patticakes

by Barbara H. Vinson

All of my cats are shorthaired, except one: Patticakes the "power puff." She's a piece of work, that one. What a comedienne! And such a pretty little thing—slate-blue, with fur like silk, and two big green eyes like emeralds.

Patticakes has an interesting background. A man came home from work one day to find her on his porch giving birth to a litter of kittens. When she was finished, he carefully transported her and her babies to a private animal shelter. Patticakes nursed her babies, and then when someone brought in some abandoned kittens, she nursed those as well.

My friend Sue adopted Patticakes as a companion for her cat. Patticakes would have been perfectly satisfied there, but unfortunately, Sue's old dog was scared to death of Patticakes. Patticakes wanted to play with him, but the old dog thought she was on the attack and just stood there, terrified, shaking in his boots. In the end, Sue called me and asked if I'd take Patticakes, and, of course, I did.

Well, Patticakes settled in for a second time and quickly won over my crew because she is so outgoing. She's hilarious to have around, whether she is stalking leaves, running full speed up a tree, or throwing herself in a snowdrift. She keeps us all laughing.

They do say laughter is the best medicine, right?

Laughter is the antidote to many vices. Genuine laughter that does not injure others cleanses the heart.

Taming Tiger Lily

by Jackie S. Brooks

I first saw Tiger Lily sitting at my garden gate, looking longingly at the house. She obviously was aware that there were other cats living here. A beautiful longhaired ginger and white kitten, about three months old and with such a sweet face—I just knew she was meant to come and live with us. Being a feral, she was quite nervous, but eventually, I was able to persuade her to come into the kitchen to eat. As soon as she saw the food, she turned and ran off. I was puzzled, until she came back with her mother in tow. Riba, as we named her mother, settled in with no problem, so Tiger Lily naturally followed her mother and happily settled in.

We already had quite a family of cats, but there was no problem at all; they accepted Tiger Lily and Riba as part of our family, too. Riba was already pregnant again and soon gave birth to six tiny kittens that she insisted belonged in a basket in the living room.

Unfortunately, Riba died of feline pleurisy some months later. It took about a year for Tiger Lily to totally trust us; until then, she would not let anyone pet her.

Tiger Lily is nearly fourteen years old now and still with us. She loves attention and can't seem to get enough of it, either from us or from her best friend, our male cat Timmy. They cuddle up close as she washes his face and ears. Quite a change from the nervous kitten she once was!

Home is the place we return to after traveling the "wilderness of the world." There we find comfort and solace among loved ones.

The New Kitten

by Carol Osborne

A customer had purchased a little male kitten from me, and it turned out to be a spoiled but lovable boy.

Approximately a year later, the lady and her husband wanted a second kitten, a little female. I gave all the usual instructions concerning the introduction of a new kitten into the household, and was told that it wouldn't be necessary because they had had a talk with the little male and he knew that he had to take care of his new sister. *Oh, sure,* I thought, but said nothing.

On the day of delivery, I took the kitten in her carrier and walked through the door, where the lady was sitting with the male on her lap.

I asked where she wanted the kitten, and she explained that the male understood and that I could just open the carrier door and he would show her around. I opened the door and braced for fisticuffs at the very least. To the contrary, that little male jumped down and led his new sister around, showing her the food and water, the litter, and then all over the house. After the tour, they settled down for a nap. I was left at the door with my mouth open. If I hadn't seen it, I would never have believed it!

Never despair of training your children or your pets. They may surprise you yet!

3

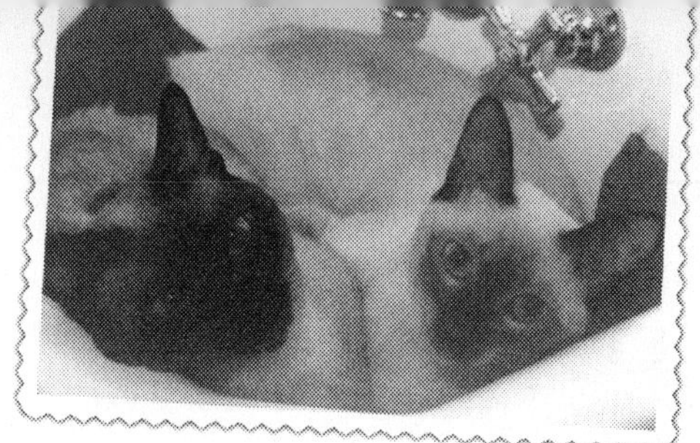

The Irresistible Cat

Getting Along with Others

Getting along with others requires the practice of many virtues, and that's a never-ending developmental process. We all make resolutions on various occasions, such as birthdays and New Year's Day. It's useful to take a good look at yourself and honestly assess what may be lacking, but more to the point, if you want to get on well with people, don't be too quick to excuse yourself and accuse others. Make those necessary and serious resolutions to improve yourself. It takes real courage to do that kind of introspective housecleaning.

Good examples are always uplifting and encouraging. Every time we see something particularly inspiring in others, we should take stock and move forward toward the same virtue in ourselves. Resolve and perseverance in personal growth add luster to our lives no matter how old we may be. The rewards are well worth the effort, and the fact is that getting along with others is what life is all about. Cats know how to make themselves utterly irresistible. Maybe we can learn a thing or two from them.

Daisy

by Barbara H. Vinson

Picture, if you will, an exquisite little blue-eyed, round-faced kitty with silky fine white fur. Superimposed on this whiteness is a "color wash" of delicate tan, mauve, and peach—as though she were a living watercolor. She has black tabby stripes on her face and legs and wears a peach-colored "necklace." Her tail is thick and plushy and brindled with alternating color. Just before its tip is a whitish ring, and the tip itself is black—as though it had been dipped in ink. She is a little masterpiece of color and design.

That's our Daisy. About a year ago, a friend of mine found her wandering around the yard and brought her to me. One look at that little beauty and it was instant adoption!

I subsequently learned that Daisy is half Siamese, so she's a talker. Once she gets started, don't expect to get a word in edgewise. Her personality is like spun sugar, but did she ever surprise me one day! Sunny, my red tabby, was teasing her, as he is wont to do with the girls. Daisy spun around, and with a mini-*roowww* smacked him soundly across his handsome orange nose. She informed him quite emphatically that he might be twice her size, but she wasn't going to put up with any of his shenanigans!

Well, if Sunny appreciates his girls with a little spunk, he's certainly more than met his match in Miss Daisy! They are now fast friends.

Be frank and direct about your feelings. A genuine friendship must be built on truthfulness.

Copy Cat

by Theresa Mancuso

Fran Nickerson has been a devoted Tonkinese breeder and show person for many years. It was a pleasure to visit her home some years back and meet her beautiful Tonkinese felines as well as a guest of honor, a handsome Siamese of the new variety, who shared quarters in Fran's home, a gentleman of honor.

Called away from the living room to answer the telephone, Fran left me in the company of several Tonks and this tubular (in this case, pronounced *tub*-ular) Siamese. I seated myself at the lovely grand piano and began to play Chopin's Nocturne in E Flat. Immediately, the elegant Siamese gentleman took his place beside me on the piano bench. He watched me and I watched him as I played.

Lifting my hands from the wrist, as my old piano teacher had shown me many years ago, I was amazed to see the Siamese cat lift one of his paws in exactly the same manner. He poised his kitty fingers above the keyboard just as I came down with another cadence of Chopin. The cat did likewise. I struck my notes and the music flowed; he struck his and a sole note resounded. Pleased with himself, the gentleman cat looked up at me as if to say, "I can do it, too."

We teach more by example than in any other way, so always be kind, forthright, and compassionate, especially in dealing with children and pets.

Dinky the Cat

by Yvette Piantadosi

Dinky's life with us started off on a bizarre note and stayed that way. The kids found Dinky in the playground one day, a lost kitten with plenty of places to hide. Once he realized that we were trying to catch him, the game of "cat and mouse" began. He was a good escape artist, so finally we gave up and sat down for lunch. Along came Dinky, rubbing up against our ankles. As soon as we got him home, Dinky became king of the castle.

We have dogs, but he paid them no mind. Whenever the dogs approached Dinky, he licked them. If they got out of hand, Dinky's fast swat taught them a lesson. When our first litter arrived, Dinky watched from his perch above the whelping box. Our new canine mom wasn't too happy about it, but since he was part of the family, she didn't chase him away.

When we took the dog outside to go to the bathroom, imagine our surprise to find Dinky with the puppies, licking them clean. The feline nanny would jump out of the whelping box for Mom, but kept watch all day and evening, waiting for a chance to get back with the puppies. He'd lie down and let them attempt to nurse on him while he cleaned their faces. As they matured, Dinky allowed the pups to chase him. He'd teach them correct cat manners when they caught him. Five years old now, Dinky still awaits his chance to take over as nanny every time we have a new litter.

Sometimes you may be of service in the most unexpected of ways, and this will cement friendships that otherwise might be thought quite unlikely.

Kitten Antics

by Lillian Howell

I would like to say that we chose a kitten, but he chose us. Prince was a confident kitten with attitude. He was the only kitten at the re-homing center that would boldly stay on your knee. He just assumed you wanted him there. And that kind of persistence pays off. We took him home, along with another kitten called Duke.

We were warned about Prince's strange habit of climbing up your leg and clinging on at feeding time—impatience I suppose. You could end up walking around with a kitten stuck to your trousers. My neighbor wasn't impressed when the kitten showed off this feat. It was his own fault for standing in the kitchen and ignoring Prince, a kitten that wanted to be noticed. After all, a kitchen is where a cat can demand feeding at any hour of the day. You can't ignore a cat gently and persistently rubbing round your legs, because when you try, you always end up tripping over him. Cats know this.

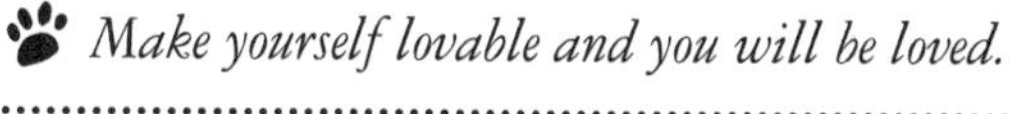

Make yourself lovable and you will be loved.

Bobbie Bobtail

by Barbara H. Vinson

Bobbie is a Jellico cat—black and white—and just a bit feral, but I think she wishes she weren't when she sees me making over the other cats. She is so cute you want to pick her up and just squeeze her and plant lots of kisses on the top of her head, but Bobbie's not into being picked up and squeezed or kissed—it's not her style. However, Bobbie is friendly enough in her own way; she's just unsure how to express it. It's as though part of her wants to trust and the other part can't quite do it.

Bobbie Bobtail literally has a bobbed tail—a little stump that she waves around like a banner. Actually, she looks fetching without a tail—it somehow suits her. A Manx cat doesn't usually have a tail, though some of them are "stumpies" like Bobbie. Maybe Bobbie is a Manx and we don't know it. One of her most charming features is a marking that makes her look as though she's wearing a black World War II bomber helmet, unfastened off to one side of her little black chin. I wish Bobbie weren't quite so reticent, but she does try in her own way to be sociable. At least I think she likes her life; she *seems* very content. I love her dearly just because she's Bobbie, but then, to *know* Bobbie is to love her!

Trust comes with time and patience.

A Wandering Cassanova

by Brenda Colbourne

When all of my other cats were in the house, I would let Cassanova go outdoors. One evening, Cassanova didn't come home, but we assumed he'd be there early the next morning. After four days our cat still hadn't come home, so I made all of the usual phone calls, which led to someone giving me yet another phone number to call. The young man on the line gave me his address, and to my surprise, it was only half a mile away! On my arrival, he greeted me and pointed to a cat relaxing in the front garden. "That's him!" I exclaimed, incredibly relieved. Cassanova looked at me graciously, unperturbed. He was simply doing what handsome toms do—getting on about town.

Experience has taught me to run my hands (and eyes) over a cat to search for wounds or an abscess when they've been missing for several days. I found an abscess above his left eye, and I was able to deal with it properly before putting him into his carrier and loading him into the car. He wouldn't be allowed outside again!

Nevertheless, Cassanova remained a happy, loving, and affectionate cat that was always pleased to see everyone. He loved all the kittens that started to arrive at our place around that time, and he was a great example to them, once we tamed his wanderlust.

The more you go out into the world, the more you'll learn the social graces that make it easy to get along with people.

Flute

by Patricia Clements

For years I've worked with rescues. Ferals are my forte, as are abandoned domestics gone wild. A local feral named Flute started surveying us—the animals and me—from two fields away and gradually moved closer. Finally he came to feed with the residents and proceeded to take over. He regularly bashed any animal rash enough to try to befriend him or share his dish.

Flute lived nearby on a farm with four not-very-nice children, and nothing more than an unfortunate mouse for tea. He wasn't neutered. I worried about my gang of twenty cats, but was reluctant to shoo him off when all he wanted was company and a kind word. I formed a cunning plan.

I encouraged Flute to eat with my cats in a mobile shelter. He'd pop in cautiously to snatch a morsel, and when he got used to it and felt no threat, I put his food in a trap. Hunger got the better of any misgivings he might have and in he went. Caught! Off to the vet and back again minus two vital parts. It was a gamble, and perhaps a bit naughty, but I knew his owners would never have him "done." Now we're all happy and I'm sure no one will ever notice that he has been altered.

Sometimes you must step in and meddle with your neighbors' affairs.

A Gentleman and a Gangster

by Theresa Mancuso

The cobby look of British shorthairs long attracted me, and finally I acquired a perfect Brit of my own. I named him after the Italian-Jewish scientist, Primo Levi, but added a distinctive flavor to his handle, calling him Il Primo di Tutti Gatti, Finalmente Arrivato (The First of All Cats, Finally Arrived), or Primo for short. From the moment he walked out of his carrier, Primo had the unerring qualities of a true gentleman. About a year later, I adopted a red tiger named Marmaduke Rodgers, a shelter cat, who is the smartest, most fearless creature I've ever known—but, truth be told, possessing the unmistakable genes of a gangster.

Marmaduke waylays Primo every chance he gets. There's a little tail action between them, and then the drama explodes, from posturing with silently insulting insinuations to screeching, hissing, striking, leaping, and rough wrestling. Abby, my German shepherd, runs to the rescue of his adopted son Marmaduke and dispatches the innocent Primo from her dear little Fauntleroy, who can do no wrong, in her opinion. My gentleman Brit soars to a high point of safety while Mother Abby encircles wildman Marmaduke with tender canine caresses. Cats *do* tolerate dogs. Some felines, like Marmi, love being loved by their canine companions. They use them, abuse them, and conquer their hearts. But gentlemen cats, like Primo, step aside graciously and wait their turn.

Mutual respect is necessary for getting along with others.

Sleeping with George

by Louise Maguire

The only dog my kitten George knew was Mutley, a laidback Doberman that he treated alternately as sparring partner and adopted parent. Mutley's ears were used for swings, and his flank was perpetually damp from George's hopeful suckling.

The visiting collie, Sally, was a nervous type, however. That behavior was caused by people, not cats, but it boosted George's morale to no end when Sally cowered from his thuggish advances on her plumy tail, retreating behind an armchair.

Sally didn't forgive his liberties. Her delayed revenge came the next day when George had to be rescued from her jaws. Released, George shot into my bedroom, taking refuge for the rest of Sally's stay. There and then I gained a furry bedfellow, who hummed like fifty fish tanks, vainly trying to suckle my hair while his front paws pounded my neck like jungle drums.

Friendships start in all kinds of ways. Be open to every new presence that enters your life and look carefully before you decide what you'll keep and what you'll discard.

Cat People

by Rod Marsden

Emily was a difficult feline. Her owners had gone to a great deal of trouble putting together a comfy open box with lots of blankets, toys, and food. So where do you think she chose to give birth to her kittens? Right on top of Phil's brand-new shirt, tie, good trousers, and coat that Diana had laid out on the lounge for him.

Poor Phil had to go to work in old jeans, a black T-shirt, and leather jacket. His sales partner was not impressed. Neither were his new clients—until he started to explain. A woman—she must have been in her fifties, and a sterner, crustier old duck you never saw—stood up and said, "So you're a cat person, are you?"

Phil nodded in the affirmative.

"Well, then," said the old duck, her face breaking into a smile. "You can't be all bad," and she reached out her hand to shake his. "No, I suppose he can't," said the old rooster beside her. "Now, let's hear about what you can do for our business."

Like-minded folks always find one another.

Tiger Meets His Match

by Louise Maguire

I sympathized when abused Tiger moved in next door, a pitiful scrap of rescued cat. Unfortunately, as he recovered from his early trials, he gradually turned into a gross tabby tyrant. Worse, my collies, Cindy and Juli, became his favorite victims.

Tiger terrorized the gentle pair, who were trained to respect felines. He ambushed them from rose beds and pounced on them from windowsills. We were soon denied the shared garden.

The big cat occupied our front steps, laying deliberate siege whether we wanted in or out. If we politely retreated, he dashed round to the back door and lurked behind the dustbins, waiting to threaten us. Our communal hall became forbidden territory whenever Tiger prowled the stairs. My collies could scarcely take refuge, trembling on their own doormat while I turned my key. Ferociously, he humped and cursed at them.

Even without their company I found myself treated as an honorary canine, hissed at and menaced.

Then, as fate would have it, my brother's eighteen-pound toy spaniel, Lady, came as a holiday guest. Now, Lady has no respect for cats and delights in keeping her own garden clear of trespassers. First thing, she chased Tiger three times around our block of apartments. When he retreated to a garden seat, up bounced Lady, too. She dusted off her paws after that enjoyable round and strolled back to report to the wide-eyed collies, Cindy and Juli, and me.

'Tis best to learn the fine art of getting along with others, rather than the difficult challenge of outsmarting the bigger bully.

Through Canine Eyes

by Bridget Quest Fulfilled (and Louise Maguire)

I lead an underdog's life now that chunky black Puma and tiny tortoiseshell Purdie have moved into the apartment upstairs.

My Human Pet confuses me. Once, she dragged me clear of all felines and snarled if I just looked at them. Now she deliberately marches me on leash up to the double temptation on our front doorstep, growling, "Leave the Kitties!" I am leaving the Kitties. She's the one disturbing the layabouts. Why are cats never told to "leave the doggies?" I make sure her legs are between me and those eight sets of daggers on display.

You never saw a cat so temptingly squirrel-like as skinny little Purdie. She hangs about deliberately outside my guard-dog window. And climbs my tree. And kills birds and dissects them for fun.

Today I thought my canine pal Max might appreciate a wag, and so I shot through our front door while my Pet was hampered by a watering can. Lazy Puma was sunbathing on the doorstep. He dithered whether to scamper away, aim for home, or shoot up my tree.

Surely someone who bounds that fast wants a race? Especially challenging a speedy canine like me! So when his tail vanished round the corner, I followed. I heard my Pet shouting, but decided she was applauding my fancy gaited style. And I didn't hurt Puma a bit. Once he was tucked out of the way under a car, I re-called and he came most obediently.

That's more than what naughty Puma and Purdie do at nightfall!

It all depends on how you look at things. Perspective is all.

How Primo Rules the Roost

by Theresa Mancuso

Primo passes judgment on everyone that crosses the threshold of our home. He scans them like Norton and McAffee, watching from his perch with big round copper-colored eyes. Sometimes, when four-leggeds visit, Primo walks right up to them, and regardless of their size, checks them out nose-to-nose. He sniffs and considers, then walks away, aloof and confident.

Primo seems to view his position in the pack as the overseer of everything I do. Writing this book has been a singular achievement, what with the large gray paws of a British shorthair wrapped around my left hand and his big round head resting on my wrist. Have you ever tried to type with such expert guidance? Primo bumps his head against mine when he wants some loving, or just flatly pounces on the newspaper and puts his whole face in my face and purrs relentlessly. I surrender and scratch his big jowls. If the cat box needs an extra scooping, Primo refuses to enter it until he has duly escorted his handmaiden and slave (me) to fulfill my duty and make it fresh and clean for the Big Boss Cat. BBC that he is, Primo does not complain unless duty obliges him for the sake of others in the pack, such as when an additional can or two or three of Fancy Feast are desired an hour after supper has been eaten. A totally irresistible guy, I am quick to obey his every wish, and why not? He's my prince.

An ounce of honey works better than a gallon of vinegar to get what you want, so keep yourself on the sweet side of things.

Riley

by Barbara H. Vinson

Dear Riley, named for the Hoosier poet James Whitcomb Riley, was one of my fosters when I lived in New York. Within a week, I had fallen in love with him and paid Patty his adoption fee because I didn't want to part with him. I believe Riley came from somewhere in Queens, and he and his two brothers were found in a junkyard. It was Patty's hunch that they must have belonged to an elderly person who either passed away or was sent to a nursing home. The relatives, not knowing what to do with the cats, simply tossed them out to fend for themselves. If this were indeed the case, it was a cruel and exceedingly stupid decision on their part, but such is the mentality of some people when it comes to animals.

Riley is such a sweetheart. He must be about fourteen years old by now, but is in gorgeous condition and looks nowhere near his age. I call him my "pastel pussycat" because he is a very pale salmon color, trimmed in white. He has beautiful deep golden eyes and an equally as beautiful disposition. I adore him.

Riley is happily lazy and peace-loving by nature, and he purrs for all he's worth when I rub his snowy white belly. That's what he thinks life is all about—having your belly rubbed and curling up with your buddies for a nice afternoon snooze.

Certainly beats the junkyard circuit!

Giving someone your love can only make your life better.

Acorn

by Susan M. Ewing

You can't have too many friends, and everyone is family. That is Acorn's philosophy. Acorn is a shorthaired orange cat that lives next door to a vacation cottage where he is the unofficial greeter.

Our first visit there, we didn't see Acorn right away, but we knew there was a cat in the neighborhood because of a note on the back bedroom window. It read, "Do not open this window or cats will come in at night and jump on your bed."

While we were there, we also discovered that the hall window was fair game. It has a wide stone sill, and one night, Acorn made the leap from roof to sill and then into the house. Acorn loves people. If I walk into the backyard, it's only a moment before I hear Acorn coming. He's very talkative. I imagine he's saying, "Wait for me, wait for me." He trots across the lawn, tail straight up, and I wait by the picnic table for him so he can jump up and be at the right level for petting. When I head back to the cottage, Acorn jumps down and runs ahead, and then throws himself down on the sidewalk, inviting me to scratch his stomach. Once I'm indoors, he waits on the walk to see if there's a chance I'll come out again.

Acorn's loving ways make us feel welcome. He may not be allowed in the cottage, but he's welcome in our hearts and we, apparently, in his.

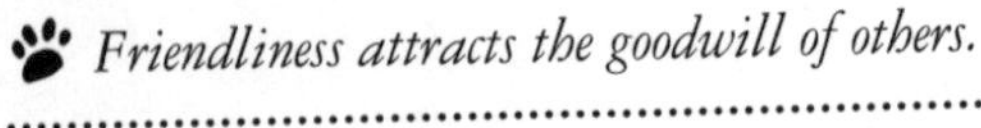

Friendliness attracts the goodwill of others.

Emerald

by Rod Marsden

It was on St. Patrick's Day that her majesty strode into a quaint Irish pub in the heart of Sydney, Australia. The barman and barmaids tried to shoo her away, but she wouldn't go and there were plenty of places to hide. Besides, they were busy pulling Guinness. As day turned to evening, the ladies and gents crowded around the storyteller in the poet's corner with its plush chairs, and they found her majesty under the storyteller's feet. The storyteller was reading from an old battered volume of *Ulysses* by James Joyce, and his burr and the cat's purr blended, sounding so lovely that no one had the heart to pick her up and toss her out.

Despite her hazel eyes, everybody called her Emerald after the Emerald Isle. To forestall any future confusion, the cat was given a collar with a dainty green stone in the center. To this day, on St. Patrick's Day, folks go to that pub to hear the man's burr and the cat's purr and to wonder what Joyce was on about.

If you find the place you belong, you'll find the natives friendly.

A Cat for All Seasons

by Jackie S. Brooks

Hey, I'm a Caruso, the "singing" Persian cat, NOT the "swimming" Turkish cat! Just what made my people think I wanted to go for a cruise on that riverboat?

We were on our way across the U.S.A., from California to Washington, D.C., prior to leaving for Merry Olde England. I must admit it was very hot that day when we arrived in Memphis, Tennessee. My folks decided they wanted to take a trip down the wide Mississippi in one of those big old riverboats, but being good people, they didn't want to leave me sweltering in the

Cadillac. Well, they got permission from the "powers that be" to take me on board. On went my harness and lead and off we went. I actually got to "walk the gangplank," so to speak, *and* I didn't have to use up one of my nine lives to do it!

In spite of my natural dislike of water, I actually had quite a good time. My folks walked me around the decks where I received lots of admiration, attention, and smiles from the other passengers. "Oh, what a cute kitty!"—I never tire of hearing that.

Going down river wasn't so bad after all. There was a nice cooling breeze, and I got to sit on a table and watch the passing scenery. Of course, out came the camera, and they just had to take more photos of me, as I am, quite naturally, very photogenic.

Ah well, pose and look superior!

How sweet it is to have the attention and affection of those we love with a few others thrown in to boot! Strive to be worthy of it!

The Irresistible Cat

by Lorraine Williams

Members of my science fiction writing group often meet for a session at my house. StarGirl, the Siamese, wanders out to greet them with a live long and prosper—I should never have let her watch *Star Trek.*

Paul is the only member of the group who can take cats or leave them. He never really gives StarGirl the time of day, whereas the other guys adore her. They get down on hands and knees to vie for her attention, calling, "Here, StarGirl-StarGirl-StarGirl." They're cat people. They own cats. They smell of cat. They're covered with cat fur. SF folk talk about furry fandom at length. They write stories about it. There's no earthly reason why StarGirl shouldn't go up to one of them.

But whom does she pick? *Wheeeeeeee . . . I want your lap!* StarGirl lands on Paul in one lovable leap. He sits there, trying to pretend to all of us, who are riddled with jealousy because we weren't chosen, that he doesn't mind all that kissing and smooching while he tries to read aloud from his masterpiece about terraforming Mars.

StarGirl accompanies Paul to the door when he leaves.

"Unrequited love," I murmur to her. "You'll get over it."

Never! StarGirl stares longingly at the door. She sighs. *I'm going to sit right here, solidly, forever, until Paul comes back.*

"Crunchies," I call out.

She bounds over to her bowl.

"Paul might come back," I remind her.

Take a message, StarGirl says, and buries her head in her food.

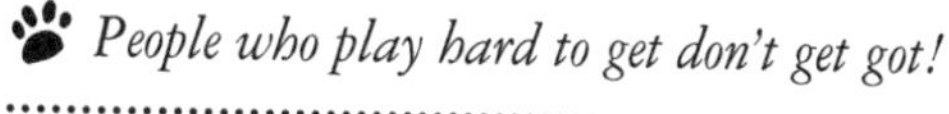

People who play hard to get don't get got!

Shandler and Islip Come to Stay

by Elli Matlin

When I first saw Shandler, a beautiful solid black kitten, he was with another baby kitten, a gray tiger stripe. I was highly allergic to cats, but I went out and bought them a can of cat food before I went home. I came back the following week and the gray kitten was gone, but Shandler was hanging around the cars in the parking lot—not a bright thing to do since we were all there with large working dogs. But Shandler kept coming up to us and rubbing against our ankles. I felt sorry for him and took him home, thinking it would be only temporary, until I could take him to the vet and put him up for adoption. At the time, my veterinarian had a batch of other kittens that needed adopting, so he said to hold onto Shandler until he had room for another kitten. After a few days, it was obvious that I couldn't give him up.

Islip is a kitten rescued from an Islip, Long Island, animal shelter where he was to be put down because he was so ill. As sleek and elegant as my Shandler is, that's how rough and tumble Islip is. Shandler is aristocracy and Islip is more like trailer trash. When Shandler jumps on the bed, you can hardly feel it, but when Islip leaps up, he must land on you, and with such a force you'd think you were being hit by a thirty- or forty-pound creature.

Respect for individual differences enables us to live and work with others.

....

How Penny Got Named

by Fran Pennock Shaw

At age nine, I bought myself an Easter duckling. My mom fretted and my dad wouldn't stop talking about duck soup, roast duck, and duck à l'orange. Yvonne stayed three weeks until she grew big as a goose. Fearing that she would end up as dinner,

I gave her to the children's zoo. I missed her terribly and my only consolation was knowing that my parents felt guilty. Thinking that any animal would cheer me, they decided I should visit my cousin Karen, who had a cat.

I knew that no *cat* could ever replace Yvonne, especially not Penny, a regular fraidy cat, who always hid under my cousin's bed. While Karen and I spent the first day in her bedroom playing, the only sign of Penny was an occasional rustling of the bed ruffle. I slept that night without once hearing padded footsteps. At breakfast, I entered the kitchen and caught a glimpse of departing copper-toned fur.

Older and wiser at eleven, Karen decided that we should ignore Penny while we talked and played where she could hear our voices, and gradually Penny emerged. Eventually, she settled near me. By day three, she was letting me pet her and meowing for more. At the end of my stay, Karen surprised me by having a "baby-naming" ceremony. The Siamese was forever after called Penny Yvonne M'Love Weinberg.

Loved ones can't be replaced, but new connections can help us heal.

....

Getting On with Fish and Dogs

by Lillian Howell

Prince liked to make himself known and so he visited the neighbors, presumptuously waiting on their doorsteps, then rudely darting in when the door was opened. Once, he visited a friend's house. She likes gardening, and gardeners tend not to like cats. They use flowerbeds as toilets—the cats, that is. Apparently, Prince snuck in while she was setting the alarm to go out. Two hours later on her return, he shot out. No damage done, except for some suspicious drips of water around the goldfish bowl. The fish was alive, but unfortunately died several days later. She wasn't sure how to dispose of the body. I volunteered Prince's services because he likes fish, but she didn't seem keen on it. And she still doesn't like cats.

Now we share Prince with another family. They bribed him with tuna. When they got a Doberman puppy, I thought Prince's visits would cease. Instead, when they were introduced at the back door, Prince backed off and went around to the front door, claiming his territory. He brought the pup to heel with a paw swipe to establish dominance. Now they lie down together and the Doberman licks Prince as much as he allows.

Prince's latest feat was turning a well-known furniture store into a pet delivery service. The sofa had to go back and so did the cat. They were very good about bringing him home after catching him. Luckily, they knew where he came from.

One man's treasure is another man's pest! Keep your pets where they belong.

4

No Hissing or Scratching, Please

The Importance of Interpersonal Communication

Cats have wonderful ways of communicating how they feel about themselves and the world around them. They never seem to doubt their own superiority or magnificence, and they have opinions about everything with no reluctance in expressing them. Living with felines is an adventure in communication. One of life's great pleasures is to watch and listen to our feline friends as they teach the important art of interpersonal communication. Sometimes, a fierce hiss with teeth apparent and ears wide apart might be necessary, but usually it's the sweet sound of purring that tells us all is well. Posture also communicates the feline mood. When a cat's tail twitches and its ears move back and forth as he crouches, something is amiss. Get ready for aggressive behavior that might be playful or serious depending on the situation. Kittens removed from the nest too young often try to suckle your finger or knead on your body or an item of clothing. This kneading might continue into adult life, a carryover from kneading on their mothers while nursing. In every kind of relationship, interpersonal communication is an art. Words, facial expressions, gestures, and postures speak volumes. Learn from the cat to say your piece intelligently, honestly, and persuasively. Be willing to listen respectfully when others do, too.

Cat Story

by Pam Fuoco

My experience with cats has been very limited. In Nashville last year, while visiting my nephew and his wife, John and Michelle, I met Marilyn, their cat. Marilyn had adopted John and Michelle in Las Vegas nine years earlier. They were her ticket to the "good life," so she moved right into their apartment, forcing them to move to a new place when the landlord refused to allow Marilyn to stay. From the start, Queen Marilyn took over and ruled the Hosp household with an iron paw.

One time I was visiting, and John said he'd be downstairs in his office and that if Marilyn started acting strange, it was probably near her feeding time. An hour later, I was reading in the living room. Marilyn was watching the birds from her window perch. Suddenly, she jumped down and ran to me. She looked at me and made a mad dash into the kitchen. I kept reading. She did it again. I kept reading. The third time, I got up and followed her. When she sat in front of her bowl and I said, "I guess you wanna eat," Marilyn thumped her tail affirmatively. "I don't know where your food is. Go get John." I felt foolish talking to a cat. Marilyn raced downstairs, returning with John right behind her.

This might be routine for cats, but I was amazed that Marilyn could communicate her needs even better than some humans.

We communicate by words, looks, and gestures. Becoming a good communicator will ensure that you get your wants and needs met properly and on time.

....

A Message Sent Zazu Style

by Sharon Ulrich

Zazu was a ratty-looking orange and white tabby cat with a misshapen tail, scarred ears, and enough attitude to fill the body of a tiger. When Zazu first arrived at the newly opened Mae Bachur Animal Shelter, he seemed like any other streetwise stray. He didn't have a fancy pedigree, he started catfights for fun, and he definitely didn't come when he was called. But Zazu was a charismatic guy, and we soon became fond of his endless energy and kitty cuddles. It was obvious that Zazu adored people, and he was horribly upset each night when everyone went home and left him alone.

Like any new building, the shelter had a few problems to work out, and the most annoying glitch seemed to be embedded in the alarm system. After everyone had left each night, the motion detector alarm would be triggered, and I'd have to return. Zazu was always extremely pleased to have a midnight visitor.

One evening I shut Zazu in his room early, and the case of the faulty alarm was solved when I witnessed a perfectly balanced and surprisingly dexterous Zazu opening his own door. He would never come to us when we called, but this clever fellow had discovered a foolproof way to make us come to him every time.

Often, it's not what you say but how you say it that delivers the message loud and clear.

Seeing the Light

by Lyn McConchie

It was evening, and as usual, I switched on the bedside lamp and settled down with a book, crocheting, and TV for the evening. Several hours later, Tiger, my Ocicat, wandered up on the bed. Halfway toward me he developed a fixed look, then stalked slowly forward and off to one side. Craning his neck like a giraffe, Tiger leaned forward to sniff the bedside lamp, jerking his whiskers back very quickly just before he touched it, and began squawking at me. My eyebrows rose. I've had cats most of my life. I know that signal.

Gingerly I advanced my hand and then matched Tiger's withdrawal. The lamp was too hot to touch. I switched it off hastily and left it for half an hour to cool. Later, I switched it back on with a lower watt bulb, but after an hour it was almost red-hot again. I turned it back off, unplugged it, and removed it to the kitchen for safe disposal.

The next day I puttered off on my electric mobility scooter to our village crafts shop and bought a new lamp. It's a lucky thing Tiger has such endless curiosity. Fortunately for me, I've had cats so long I can translate feline body language. Usually that particular lamp would be left on, sometimes for several hours while I was not in the bedroom. Without Tiger, there would most likely have been a fire.

Body language is just as important as words in the communication of mood and idea.

....

The Kitten That Almost Got Me Slapped

by Ed Kostro

A few years back, I rescued a tiny black kitten that I found abandoned in a restaurant parking lot while on a business trip a thousand miles from home. He looked like he really needed a friend.

I placed the little guy in a small black vinyl carrier and attempted to sneak him into my NO PETS ALLOWED hotel. I put the bag under my arm and nonchalantly strolled into the elaborate hotel lobby. No one suspected a thing.

As I approached the elevator to head up to my room, a rather attractive-looking woman strolled up beside me. I innocently said, "Good evening." She responded in kind. After we entered the elevator, it seemed like it took an eternity to reach her floor. As she finally began walking out the door, I breathed a sigh of relief. She hadn't suspected a thing either.

That's when my tiny friend in the bag made an extremely loud noise that I can only describe as the best male "catty come on" I've ever heard. *RROWWWW!*

The woman immediately spun around and gave me the nastiest glare I have ever seen. If looks could kill, I would have dropped dead on that elevator floor. My embarrassment was unbearable.

After I finally reached the safety of my room, I chewed out my new little feline friend rather severely. Then I laughed hysterically, wondering if this clever kitten had a devilish sense of humor.

Beware of false security. Anything can happen—and it usually does!

Mr. Ambassador

by Theresa Mancuso

The day I brought Primo into our home as a twelve-week-old kitten who had just crossed the U.S.A. in an airplane, waited a long while at the JFK airport to be unpacked from baggage, and persevered in his good nature while we drove the long ride back to Brooklyn, you'd not perhaps expect a good mood and friendly humor. This little kitty had every reason to hiss and bristle when he stepped out of his carrier into the living room of his new home. Immediately, my two enormous German shepherds approached the kitten, eager to sniff and lick him. Ever the perfect ambassador of goodwill and brotherhood, Primo took all in his stride.

He lifted his beautiful round head to touch Grip's nose with his own. They rubbed noses for a quick moment. Then, it was

Abby's turn to greet the newcomer. Obediently taking a down position, she lay quietly waiting, allowing Mr. Ambassador to approach her, and approach he did, with all the finesse of the world traveler. That's all it took for Primo to make himself at home. In a few days' time, he was positioning himself back-to-back, lengthwise, with Grip on his pad or Abby on the futon. When friends of mine came to call, their animals in tow, Primo never hid or sought refuge elsewhere. Instead, with perfect confidence, my "big cat" stood toe-to-toe and nose-to-nose with every dog that came to visit, large and small. Perhaps, this cowboy cat was a city dude at heart, for nothing has ever phased him in his Brooklyn home.

In new situations, anticipate the best, and usually the best will happen.

....

Interfeline Communication

by Linnette Horne

Interfeline communications can be interesting to watch if one takes the time. I was witness to one exchange between my then felines-in-residence, Pretty and Rambo. Pretty was seal point Siamese, one of the English types—short and stocky with a full face, rather than the more well-known skeletal type with the ear-splitting meow.

Pretty was with us for seventeen years, and before she died of old age, she oversaw the arrival of Rambo, a brown tabby with big green eyes. Rambo arrived as a lively kitten that decided I was to be *his* human and that was that. Pretty took one look at him and recognized that this kit needed a firm paw to keep him in line. On this particular occasion, Pretty was on the bed with me and Rambo arrived, clearly wanting to join us at the pillow end, but Pretty was having no part of this idea. She put the eye on him as soon as he landed on the bed. I saw Rambo look longingly at our end of the bed and then at Pretty, but there was no arguing with her. He could stay on the bed, but only at the foot, and so it was. Pretty had made her point and all done without a single meow.

Speak softly and carry a big paw.

A Calculating Cat

by Louise Maguire

Tortoiseshell Mash is a rather private cat, not really feral, because she had a previous home before she decided the grub was tastier at her present abode. Too true she is huge—positively circular. However, she's no lap cat and doesn't much like being picked up, even by her family.

Now, a course of eye drops had to be completed while her people were away. My holiday challenge.

Thursday: She strolled into the kitchen at teatime. Wary of my simplest gesture, she bounced speedily under the dining room table. A hands-and-knees approach cracked my incautious head. Round One to Mash.

Friday: My nearest contact was an occasional brief leg caress. When I bent down to tickle her arched back, she bolted upstairs and vanished. Round Two to Mash.

Saturday: Mash let me close enough to inspect the state of her eyes, while blinking politely, feline style. I was permitted to touch her outsized fluffy tail, but getaway time swiftly followed, beneath a double bed. My arms proved too short to reach her. Round Three to Mash.

Sunday: I tracked her down on a chair back enjoying early morning sunshine. Then came the surprising sequel. I was allowed to caress her, scratch behind both ears, and rub her cheeks. I got a purring response and firm head pushes back. Enormous Mash stropping with her front paws in feline ecstasy is quite a sight.

My Round? No. More likely that cunning Mash had calculated any need for eye drops was past.

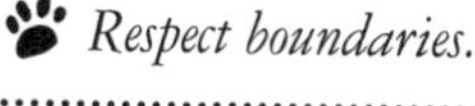

Respect boundaries.

You Can't Tell a Cat by Its Cover

by Maxine Perchuk

Sylvester Salvatore Kneivel and Isadora Bernadette Wintercorn have a typical sibling relationship. Sylvester, my big orange tabby, is the younger brother, and as such feels it is his job to annoy Isadora, my petite calico, who is half his size and a year older. Sylvester enjoys waiting until Isadora is cozily nestled by the radiator until he pounces. He barely makes contact—just enough to rouse her from her sleep and cause her to feign a swipe at him. She then retreats behind the fortress of the window guards as Bea and Willy, the canine siblings, chase Sylvester from the room.

I then comfort Isadora, who climbs on my lap, telling her it's not fair that a delicate flower like herself must be subjected to the likes of that little roughneck, and I remind her to try and be patient with her little brother. She snuggles and purrs to the validation, a gentler soul I know not. So it is with some consternation that I have come to learn that my little rose petal of a feline enjoys taunting her older sibling, Beatrice the basset, with the food on the countertop. Beatrice strains to get a stray morsel near the edge, while Isadora happily bats it away, then swallows it from a safe height.

Appearances can be deceptive.

A Dog at Cats' Pajamas

by Anna Haltrecht

Yes, I am a dog, but I'd rather be a cat. Especially living at Cats' Pajamas, where the cats are spoiled rotten. Their bowls are always full, they can come and go as they please through their own door, and they can walk all over the kitchen table. Actually, they walk all over their owner, especially when she lounges at ground level. I have found the best defense against the cats is to ignore them. But I am big and brown and I can't help wagging my tail, which they seem to be fascinated with as they attempt to bat it back and forth. They love making passes at my back end as

I slink by. Truly their favorite pastime is blocking the doorway so that I feel completely at their mercy. And then, they get all huffy by puffing themselves up and pretending that they are very huge and scary—which they are; that's the problem.

They bare their teeth and hiss. They strike out with their very sharp claws. They stare straight at me and swish their fluffy tails swiftly right and left. And then when I can bear it no longer, I hear my favorite words and my mistress saves me. "Snowball! Bamboo! Leave Daisy alone."

At last I can come into the house, get my cookie treat, and lie down by the fire in peace. Well, at least until the next time the felines have their way with me.

Accept yourself the way you are. Do not expect that everyone else will do the same; but you're your own best friend when it comes to facing adversarial alliances.

The Cordless Four-Legged Answering Machine

by John R. "Jack" Vinson

One hot summer night more than twenty years ago, my new wife and I were lying on the floor watching TV, with the front door wide open to let the cool breeze from the desert work off some of the heat in our mobile home. In through the open door walked a longhaired red tabby that seemed to say, "Hi, guys, got anything to eat?"

That was the beginning of a wonderful eighteen years we had living with our Morris. I don't have a clue where he came from since we were living in a remote area out in the New Mexico desert, but he couldn't have been a feral cat because he liked people.

Some time later, we moved to a large ranch home, where I worked out of my home office. On several occasions, it happened that my boss asked me who was answering my phone at home without saying anything. I figured the boss had just called the wrong number and gave it no mind until one morning when the phone started ringing while I was in the bathroom. As I ran around the corner into the kitchen to answer the phone, I was just in time to see Morris swat the telephone off the hook with a smug look on his face that seemed to be saying, "There, I shut that noisy thing up again."

From then on, Morris was also known as our cordless, four-legged, fuzzy answering machine!

There are many ways to avoid unwanted calls—as long as they're not from your boss.

A Catnip Tale

by Karen Heist

Two of our cats, Sammy and Sam, were upstairs with my mother in her bedroom while she was cleaning. We had a big jar of catnip that my mother moved off the shelf to dust. Meanwhile, Sammy, who is a little cat, stuck her head in the plastic jar to get at the catnip, and she got her head stuck and could not get it out. Sammy panicked and ran around the room with the jar stuck on her head.

My mother finally got the jar off of her, and Sam, who smelled the catnip on Sammy, would not leave Sammy alone the rest of the day. She ran away from him and he followed. Finally, Sammy got so mad that she hissed at him, but still he refused to back down and continued to pester her. Mom tried to chase Sam away, but he just wouldn't go. He totally refused to leave Sammy alone, so drawn was he by the delicious scent of catnip.

Finally, my mother banished poor, sort-of-innocent Sammy into a room where she could lick the catnip off of herself in peace. Sam determinedly waited just outside the door, hissing, scratching, and meowing loudly to get in.

Sometimes getting too much attention is worse than not enough.

Chippie Bandito

by Barbara H. Vinson

I once knew a lady who rescued more stray cats than she could comfortably handle and ended up with a full house! Fortunately, my friend Judy helped her place most of them, and then it was easier for her to care for those she still had.

But one little fellow had been completely overlooked. He lived in a cage and never got out to exercise. Judy asked the lady, "Why is this little guy stuck in a cage?"

The lady answered, "Because he's mean!"

"Mean?" laughed Judy. "Why, he's not mean; look at him." And sure enough, the little cat was rubbing Judy's hand with his head for all he was worth. He was so happy for a little affection.

The lady still insisted he was mean. She said she was actually thinking of having him put to sleep. Judy said, "Oh, no you don't. He's *shy*, not mean. I have a friend I am going to call about him. She favors black-and-white cats, and this one is darling with that little white bandana design around his neck and those little white whisker pads."

I'm the friend Judy called, and of course I took him! Judy was right—Chip hasn't got a mean bone in his body. He's a shy little soul, yet *so* affectionate. Our kitty household is all the better for Chip's being a part of it. I wouldn't take anything pretty in exchange for him, and I'm sure if you had him, you wouldn't either!

Beauty is in the eye of the beholder. Let love be the judge.

Brigitte

by Rod Marsden

Pat the artist's relationship with Brigitte was somewhat unique. You see, Brigitte wasn't just an artist's model; she was also a critic.

It began a year after Brigitte was presented to him as a kitten. He was enjoying a cup of coffee after a hard day when he noticed that, instead of three paintings to sell, he really only had one. The other two had great, glorious cat rips in them. What's more, he looked at the untouched painting and decided it was the worst of the three. He offered it for sale anyway and, boy, did it sell!

Brigitte was kept out of his studio for a long time after that. One day, about five years later, however, she was accidentally let in and curled up under a certain sculpture he was thinking of ditching, and she was purring. The next day he offered the sculpture to an art dealer and it sold for mega bucks!

This scratching and purring became a regular thing, and they lived together for many years. They passed away within a month of one another, proving something about artists and their most erstwhile critics.

If you fancy yourself a critic, deliver your comments in a kindly and respectful manner. The soft touch makes criticism more palatable.

An Interspecies Friendship

by Fran Pennock Shaw

My guinea pig has a new friend. That's surprising because J.J. is not a friendly fellow. He's bossy and self-centered. His cage is his castle. More astounding, J.J.'s friend is a cat. Honey, a cream and black Maine coon mix, is maybe not the smartest feline I've ever known, but certainly the most easygoing.

J.J. and Honey met when I asked Honey's parents to pet-sit for ten days. I hesitated to bring these species together, but then, I didn't have any choice—most people turn you down when you ask them to keep a rodent in their house. And after all, I knew Honey. She wouldn't hurt a bee.

I didn't count on Honey's curiosity about the cage, the cage table, the cage litter, and the cage occupant. For days, J.J. hid in a back corner, screeching invectives while the giant furball roamed below. One day, J.J. was rattling his cage bars for attention and became so absorbed that he didn't realize Honey was nearby, not until she stood up on her hind legs, stretched her paws up on the table, and came nose-to-nose with him.

My friends say there was a seemingly eternal moment of silence as the two stared at each other. Then, Honey casually returned to the floor and J.J. went about his business. Thereafter, J.J. didn't hide from Honey, who would comfortably curl up to sleep under J.J.'s table. A perfect friendship had begun.

Communication sometimes requires taking risks and making compromises. The best communicators are those who don't fall apart when such moments arise.

The Fine Art of Communication

by Lorraine Williams

I'm a very tired person. It wouldn't be so bad if StarGirl stayed at the foot of the bed. But, no, she wants the lot of it. I only have to reach across to the side table for my spectacles or to pick up the clock, and she'll push her paws out to claim more mattress. Once I was even maneuvered—thump!—onto the floor. In her opinion, it's a rather silly thought to suppose that beds are made for humans.

Well, no kitty cat was going to dictate to me. By gosh, it was time I slept alone without a furry feline in tow.

"I've had it, StarGirl," I whined. "For the rest of the night, I'm not sleeping with a cat. And that's final. No arguments, yes? *Two* of us can't fit in this bed!"

Mee-yowwwww. No arguments from me . . . StarGirl stretches out across the bed.

I finish the night on the two-seater sofa in the lounge. There, I'd shown StarGirl who was boss!

Getting one's point across is not always a simple matter of telling it like it is.

....

Jaspur's Collar

by Lauren L. Merryfield

One of the first items we bought for Jaspur after adopting him when he was eight weeks old was a collar. We got him one with a bell so that I would have a better idea where he is, since I am blind. Though some kitties rail against the collar, Jaspur not only wants his collar on, he finds ways to alert us if it comes off accidentally.

One day, when Jaspur was lying on me, I reached down and he grabbed my hand and bit it slightly. I thought this was odd, but then I realized he really wanted me to pay attention. I did.

His collar was gone. Later, I found the collar lying on the floor right in our main path near the dining room.

The following day, I again noticed that Jaspur had no collar. I asked him about it, and he rubbed my hand with his head. I said I'd find it later.

On my way out of the bathroom, I discovered the collar on the floor and went back to Jaspur, who was waiting for me as usual. He let me put it back on him with no fuss. I think I detected some accidental purring, too!

What we wear has a real effect on how we feel about ourselves, and we project that to others.

Marilyn's Secret

by John Hosp

Our cat Marilyn was primarily an outdoor cat that had been somewhat neglected before she adopted us. During the several years it took to turn her into an indoor cat, she continued to enjoy the outdoors.

One day, she was sitting looking out of the patio door making noises at the birds in the yards. One of us mistakenly opened the door and out shot Marilyn around the corner after a bird. I ran outside and around the house in time to catch up with her, bird in mouth, strutting toward the door. Our eyes met.

"Marilyn!" I said.

She stopped and sat down, still holding her prey.

"Put that down!" I scolded.

Not taking her eyes off of me, Marilyn lowered her head and released the bird, which was still alive but scared.

"Now get away from it," I said. Marilyn backed off a couple feet from her victim, never taking her eyes off of me. The bird flew off and Marilyn flinched, but she didn't chase it.

"Come here," I said, trying to sound comforting. Marilyn came. I gave her a lecture on not chasing birds, emphasizing how much we appreciated her wanting to bring it back to us.

Marilyn never chased another bird, even when one got into our house a few years later. Now we know that Marilyn understands more of what we say than she shows. When she ignores us, we say, "Look, Marilyn, we know you know exactly what we're talking about." It doesn't seem to help!

Speak out firmly in defense of the weak and helpless and listen to what others have to say.

Singing to My Cats

by Theresa Mancuso

I sing to my pets. They respond with movements and sounds of their own. It seems that each one recognizes and likes his song best of all. Here's why I think cats love being sung to.

Primo's melody is my own creation. I cannot reproduce it in this book, but the words go like this: "Il primo di tutti gatti, finalmente arrivato, Primo, Primo, Primo, Primo mio, oh Primo mio,

Oh-o Primo MiOoooo." Believe it or not, at the sound of these lyrics and my alto voice rolling out those Italian r's, my beautiful British shorthair moves the tip of his luxurious tail ever so slightly thus and so, back and forth. He looks at me and nods. Nor are my alley cats, Marmaduke and Charlie, less enthralled by my songs for them. They roll about sensuously and give me tiny kitty bites, a sign of cat love.

Maximus, my all-time favorite Siamese, was the tiniest fully grown cat I've ever seen. Her song, though not as elegant as the Primo aria, nonetheless led Max to keep time with her tail. She walked about with tail slung up proudly over her hindquarters, wriggling back and forth rhythmically. Nikki, my Tonkinese, loved her special serenade, a whisper of words sung deep and low. Whenever I sang to Nikki, she made fancy pirouettes, dancing round and round about my legs before she finally lay down on her back, offering her soft white belly to caress.

All sentient beings respond to love and affection.

HELP! An Awful Experience!

by Camilla Baird, as told by Primprau's Ditakah Pakh Di (eight-month-old male cat)

Here's how terrible it is to grow up male around here! One used to be allowed to play and romp throughout the house. Then, one day, the kitchen door is closed and one is confined to the bathroom and cellar. The floor is heated there and the stairs are fun; Bro is also there, so it's not too bad at first. One misses the attention and hates not being allowed to go out into the yard. All these restrictions just for having learned that a male must mark his territory! It doesn't even smell bad—yet!

Then, suddenly, while enjoying oneself on the heated bathroom floor, one is scooped up and screwed into a diaper! How degrading! And scary. The diaper tightens just above the hips almost paralyzing the hind legs. Bro teases and one can take that, but one can't walk in diapers and that's hard to take! One loses patience dragging around, struggling to walk without the use of hind legs, paralyzed by the diapers. Strange wild hops make it all the more frightening!

The diaper stays on. Camilla must hate that male smell, and the plant on the windowsill isn't very happy being thrown to the floor either. She takes hold of me, trying to calm me down, saying that the diaper's not so bad. I *can't* agree, so I start hyperventilating and shivering. Camilla feels sorry for me and removes the wicked diaper. Lo and behold! I can walk again!

When certain things are hard to understand, but cooperation is nevertheless required, be patient. Wait and see.

5

Feline Survival (The Nine Lives Theory)

Work as if You Only Have Today, Live as if You'll Live Forever

It's a superstition that cats have nine lives, a belief that arose because they seem to survive all sorts of mishaps, falls from high places, injuries, broken ribs, bloodied noses or mouths, cold weather, and even fatal fires and explosions, not to mention their most frequent plight, homelessness.

Nature provides cats with a great sense of balance, so they can right themselves and land on all fours, a brilliant feat! They might start upside down in a free fall, but they make an incredible adjustment and land gracefully on all fours, with the shock of impact absorbed evenly so no harm is done. Survivors! Vets report that cats do better when they fall from a high place rather than a low one. Check your physics book to learn why; I'm sure I don't know. Or maybe, ask a cat.

They are often mysterious and majestic, possessing the ability of perfect concentration when stalking a mouse or getting ready to pounce on a favorite toy. Cats almost never lose their dignity and composure. They can be stealthy and discreet in situations where you and I would bungle everything. Stalking is cat work, after all, and they do it to perfection. Wouldn't you like to land on all fours every time? Don't you wish you could concentrate when you're driven to distraction? Hey, look, maybe we don't need nine lives if we could only do it right the first time. The way cats do!

Akira, the Hunter

by Lisa Sanders

The ever-loving Akira in her wildest dreams would never have thought that she could live up to her hunter brother's legacy as a mouser. Akira is FeLV+ and has her ups and downs from the disease. Her hunting is the goofiest picture of feline prowess you'd ever see. Picture a hysterical mother, if you will, flailing her arms in panic while being taken on a roller coaster her child had said was not scary. Such a scene would help you visualize what Akira looks like trying to hunt anything.

Much to our surprise, however, Akira actually succeeded one day. All I heard was fierce growling, lots of it. I shrugged it off, figuring that brother feline, Indy, was bothering her. The commotion didn't stop, so off I went to investigate. Akira's tiny mouth was clamped down as tight as any pit bull's locked jaws, and a skinny tail was hanging from between her teeth. She was not about to give it up, not to Indy, not to me, not to anybody. After an hour of chasing my growling hunter around, trying to pry her little mouth open, I finally won, salvaging what was left of the mouse so I could go bury it.

Akira followed me, pouting until the merciful act was done. Then, she turned her back on me and walked away, still annoyed that I had taken her prize. Congratulations, fierce and noble hunter!

Never give up, even if you look foolish to others while you're trying to learn a new skill.

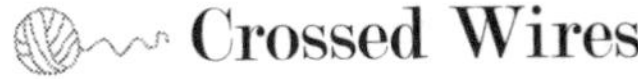

Crossed Wires

by Lyn McConchie

Recently, my phones went odd, giving a hiccup and going silent instead of ringing. The telephone repairman was a cat lover. As the repairmen crawled along the wiring, checking joins, jacks, and plugs, plugging and unplugging, and ringing the phone internally on his gear as he went, my cat Tiger couldn't believe his eyes. How great to have a visitor who got down and crawled, apparently hunting prey as Tiger did—not quite the usual guest we get around here.

Tiger crept along beside him, eyes alert for whatever prey his new friend might be seeking. Every time the repairman turned to speak to me, he found himself nose-to-nose with Tiger, who was asking if he'd seen it yet. While the man and his family have cherished cats of their own, he was obviously oblivious to just *why* Tiger was creeping along beside him so carefully the entire time.

The repairman found the fault after an hour of crawling about (corroded terminals in the original old phone in the bedroom), and he replaced it, checked everything again, and rose to go. Tiger was disappointed though philosophical; a hunt was often like that. You stalked for ages and caught nothing, but it was fun. Perhaps this nice man would come again and they might have better luck.

When there's work to be done, pitch in!

Peaches

by Barbara H. Vinson

Peaches got off to a rather precarious start in life. A woman I worked with said she needed to get a cat because there was a mouse in her apartment. She figured the cat would catch the mouse and that would be that. Because she said she hated cats, I thought it strange that she would even consider acquiring one in lieu of a good mouse trap, but sure enough, she up and got herself a kitten from the local shelter—a little brown tabby with a milky-white nose.

The woman eventually got fed up with having Peaches around. One day, she became really angry over something and grabbed the cat, throwing her out of a three-story window. For two days Peaches wandered around the building's courtyard, bewildered and traumatized.

When I found out about this from the woman's friend (who ratted on her, thank heavens), I told the woman I'd take her cat. There's a lot more I'd have liked to say but didn't want to get her dander up; she might have taken it out on the hapless creature a second time. Two days later, Peaches was mine.

Peaches is a gentle little spirit, sweet and affectionate. How that woman could have committed such evil against her I cannot fathom, but I do know that the law of cause and effect is pretty strict: She'll get hers. Meanwhile, I'm just grateful Peaches belongs to *us*—the little brown tabby with the milky-white nose.

Whatever your private beliefs may be, know this: You cannot do harm with impunity.

To Be a Cat

by Tracy Heyman

To be a cat or to be a dog? In my next life I will return as a cat, and hopefully a cat who owns a wealthy family. The reason I wouldn't return as a dog owned by a wealthy family is that I get seasick and I am sure they would expect me to go "yachting" with them regularly. Plus, I would hate to have to walk outside on cold, bitter snow in order to relieve myself. Let's face it: Cashmere booties can only do so much. To be a cat or to be a dog? To be a cat would be purrfect.

I would return as a cat, and my wealthy family would be so glad to be owned by me. They would be extremely smart and understand how important I am in their lives. I would keep them physically and emotionally healthy by extending them the honor of petting my soft, silky fur. I would also make them laugh all the time, and that, too, would be good for their health. As a cat who owns a wealthy family, I would protect our mansion better than any secret security system, and especially better than any dog. Thieves would never fool me with a juicy slab of steak. I could eat steak anytime I wanted if I owned a wealthy family. Besides, I would have claws! To be a cat or to be a dog? To be a cat is the only way.

Enjoy life's little pleasures.

One Person's Trash

by Edy Makariw

I gladly acquiesced when the vet asked me to foster a beautiful orphan kitten. Later, he called me into an examination room to show me the ugliest kitten I'd ever seen, its white coat smeared with coffee grounds and tomato sauce, head too small for its body, and eyes different sizes. It was unable to walk more than a few steps without crashing down on its face. Malnutrition or something worse was at work. Would I take this one instead of the beautiful tabby?

A woman brought the kitten into the clinic after her dog found it in a trashcan set out on the sidewalk the previous evening. As I bathed the foundling, I pondered why anyone would place a living thing in the trash.

The vet had just euthanized an old, incurably ill cat for a client who wanted another kitty immediately. He reassured me that she would provide an excellent home and brought me back to meet the bereaved woman who was chuckling through her sobs as "my" tabby batted her fingers with mini-marshmallow-sized paws. I realized the healing value of her taking "my" kitty and knew this would free me to care for the peanut butter–streaked orphan that might have no other chance.

At the end of my shift, I brought the "weird one" home. Her health and balance improved daily as she dug into her new digs, and my home and heart. She might not be perfect, but she's perfectly mine.

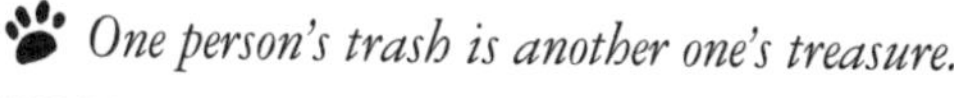
One person's trash is another one's treasure.

Locked In

by Theresa Mancuso

Maximus, a very tiny Siamese with enormous curiosity, landed on all fours when she leaped from the bureau to the bottom drawer while I was sorting socks there.

Being somewhat neurotic about the process, I was completely absorbed with arranging the socks by color and age. Peripherally, I must have seen Max, but I paid her no mind, and just as quickly, she slipped from my mind. But this stealthy Siamese burrowed under the sock pile farther and farther toward the back of the drawer.

The phone rang. I closed the drawer hurriedly and rushed into the living room to answer it. An important long-distance call soon deteriorated into an hour-plus of reminiscences and humorous anecdotes—so much for family crises. When feeding time came, only one cat alighted on the counter. Where was Max? I searched, calling her name to no avail. Terrified for her safety, I took comfort knowing that the apartment door had not been opened nor were windows unscreened. Maximus had to be *somewhere* in the place. The evening progressed; no Max, and I forgot that she was missing.

Next morning, it was time to get dressed, so I opened the sock drawer. My very hungry, but otherwise unaffected, Siamese leaped out like a rocket and hastened to breakfast.

If you are lost, remain calm and have faith that you will be found.

Alligator Wrestling

by Tina Juul

When I moved to Denmark, I took Dexter to Florida to live with my sister. In the tropics, Dexter was allowed to move in and out freely through a torn window screen, using a nearby mango tree as her gateway to freedom. I called my sister regularly to hear how my kitty was faring in the wild streets of West Palm Beach. Once, she admitted that Dexter had been gone for a few days and that when the cat came back, she was missing part of her ear. When I took the news fairly well, she revealed that this was normal behavior for my not-so-innocent cat. Dexter would go away for about a week at a time but would always show up in one piece, albeit dirty and skinnier. My sister once started a telephone conversation with "Your cat is fine, but…" followed by "…emergency surgery" and "…$300." Dexter had come home after a month with her paw caught in her collar and an abscess permeating her neck. Needless to say, that was her final outing in Florida.

We still don't know where she was during that month. We like to imagine she was wrestling alligators in the Everglades, but only because she lives with me now, not a swamp in sight. Just in case cats don't have nine lives, though, it's better that she stays in the safe confines of Denmark, far away from any alligators that might take what is most probably her last life.

If you cherish challenges and love to face the impossible, put your all into it and you'll come out just fine.

Meemers and the Fire

by Caroline McRae-Madigan

In 1990, I was living in a country home when it was destroyed by a fire. I couldn't find my Persian cat, Meemers, anywhere, and the firefighters thought she couldn't have gotten out alive. I refused to accept that possibility. It was midwinter, freezing cold, and there was a lot of snow. For two days my neighbors and I searched for her; I cried constantly. Still, I wouldn't give up. On the third day, I walked past what used to be a hot tub. I heard a faint meow.

Meemers never meowed loudly. My heart started pounding, and I called her name over and over. Sure enough, I heard her.

Meemers had escaped the fire and run across the frozen field, taking refuge in a small gap under the hot tub. The ice that was melted by the fire had refrozen. She couldn't get loose to come to me. I went to a neighbor's to get a flashlight, and we returned together. Lying on my belly, I saw Meemers frozen to the ice. She had been pinned there for days without food. We tore off two boards from the hot tub and carefully chipped away the ice around her. After two days at the vet's, Meemers was released, healthy and perfect. In several months, the hair on her belly grew back—she never complained. For the next ten years, life was great for my Meemers and me. She was never sick and never missed sleeping with me every night, glued to my shoulder.

In life's darkest moments, never give up hope.

Mukie Cat and the Insurance Salesman

by Mary Rodgers Easton

One day back in 1950, when my daughter, Mary, was only about three months old, she was sitting in her baby buggy near the screen door of our house. I had just wheeled her in from the courtyard, and Mukie Cat had followed us. He took up his post, stretched out in front of Mary's baby buggy. I had baby diapers to hang, so I went outside through the back entrance, where I could see the front door and keep an eye on both baby and cat while I worked.

A life insurance salesman came to the porch and tried to walk in the front door. In our town back then, life insurance salesmen always came to try to sell to new parents after a baby's birth was announced in the paper. I greeted him politely, and he came in.

Mukie Cat was a longhaired fellow, and while the salesman talked to me, every single hair on Mukie's body continuously stood straight up. I gently stroked Mukie, but his hair stayed up and he remained on the alert.

Five minutes into his pitch, with eyes glued on Mukie Cat, the salesman decided to retreat. "I don't really think you need insurance right now, ma'am." With that, he raced away.

If your needs are already satisfied, there's no need to tarry with salespeople.

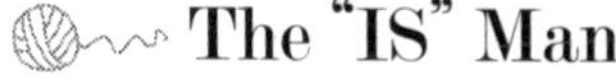

The "IS" Man

by Caroline McRae-Madigan

My cats, Casanova and Celeste, became parents of two kittens, one stillborn and one that weighed less than two ounces. We were not optimistic. We used heating pads and stuffed toys to keep the live one warm. One of the saddest things about being an only kitten is that every time Mommy leaves, there are no siblings to huddle with for warmth.

Week one and he was still with us. Week two and Mommy decided that one kitten was too boring for her. She didn't want to stay with him, so we started to bottle-feed. Celeste still fed him, too, but as soon as she was done, she would grab him by the neck, throw him in the air, slam dunk him, and then start to kick him like a toy! Someone had to be present at all times with the kitten.

We asked each other constantly, "Is he OK? Is he warm? Is he hurt? Is he hungry? Where is he?" This continued for a month until we nicknamed him "Is He." After a very slow start and many health issues due to his premature size, at three months he got to go to his wonderful new family. Sandy and Steve carried on the name Is He, but they spell it Izzy, or jokingly call him their Is Man, for he is the love of their life. Without their love, concern, and financial support, Izzy would not be.

Love is crucial for survival.

Inspector Kneivel's All-Night Vigil

by Maxine Perchuk

Detective Sylvester Salvatore Kneivel, my orange tabby, is always on the job. Nothing stops his investigative mission, and every new item that enters the home invites a full inquiry. No, nothing gets by Inspector Kneivel.

Recently, the intrepid investigator expanded the confines of his jurisdiction to include the hallway outside my apartment.

Upon my arrival at home, the lightning-quick sleuth ran out past me in a flash, and I proceeded to fall asleep in front of the TV.

In the morning when I opened the front door, he ran down the stairs and directly inside. Apparently, he had been doing all-night surveillance duty. Detective Kneivel had stationed himself at the roof landing just outside my apartment, and curiously he had a bowl of water nearby and some food. Of course, every hard-working fellow needs adequate nutrition, but certainly it piqued my own inquisitive nature (I guess it's in the genes).

The mystery was solved when I ran into the superintendent's wife, who told me about a cat that had refused to move from his position on the stairway landing (she didn't know he was on duty), so she figured the best thing she could do was to feed him. To the more faint of heart, this might have proven to be a very challenging evening, but to Detective Sylvester Salvatore Kneivel, it was all in a night's work.

No job is menial or without merit. Enjoy your work and give it your best efforts, every day, all day.

Out of the Lion's Den

by Catherine Miller

If cats could be football players, Curly would be the captain of the team. He has the muscular bulk, a thick padding of curly, peachy fur, and a swagger that won't quit. All of this is accompanied by an uncanny insistence on chasing his ball around the room, and a refusal to rest until he commandeers it over the goal line or, in his case, the edge of the water dish. Touchdown! Game over.

I know this because the ball is always in the water dish when I come home from work. I'm the one who gets to fish it out, soggy and dripping, and clean out the dish to boot.

Curly wasn't neutered until he was a year old, when I adopted him from his breeder. It could be that all the testosterone having extra time to swirl through his system helped shape him into the dominant personality he is. One thing is certain, though. He can walk into any room and all the critters in it give way. Move over, the king of the beasts has arrived. My Persian doesn't give it a second thought. He sees Curly coming and gets out of Dodge.

Your natural talents will always come to the fore if you trust yourself.

Why Charles Andrew Always Succeeds

by Theresa Mancuso

Charles Andrew came into our life straight off the street, a vagabond kitten of no particular appeal, except that it was bitter cold and he was small and hungry. In just three months following his auspicious arrival, Charlie perfected the Vedic path to success. He blossomed into a rocket scientist, firing his body to launch six to ten feet into the air from the floor up to land on his favorite plant. He is a budding fire marshal, constantly checking the stove and whatever is cooking thereon. He is already a connoisseur of Italian and Chinese food—Charlie revels in eating. How does he do it? How does a poor cat from the streets of Brooklyn rise so swiftly in the pack? It seems to me the reason that Charles Andrew Shen accomplishes whatever he sets out to do is because he faithfully adheres to the path of success laid out in the ancient sacred scriptures of India. Charlie has mastered the way.

Put a chair in his way; he will scale it. Stack dishes on the counter between stove and sink; he will skillfully maneuver with a new strategy of approach. Hide articles you don't want Charlie to mess with; he will persevere in locating them, and when you tire of guarding the treasure trove, Charles will make off with the buttons, keys, gloves, and other items pursued in his lust for stuff. Masterful cat of the road, little Charlie is an old soul.

If you wish to succeed, strive to acquire these qualities praised in the ancient Vedas: proper effort, perseverance, courage, knowledge of the given pursuit, skill and resources, and the capacity to overcome obstacles.

Cat Missing

by Paul Sutton

If you've ever had an animal that has gone missing, you will understand the torment my family went through several years ago when one of our beloved Siamese cats disappeared. Silver and his sister Saffi were my late Mum's pride and joy, and we kept them as house cats because she was terrified of losing them and they were frightened of going outdoors. I can't remember how Silver got out, but I'm still aware of the trauma I felt when he went missing. We were distraught. We searched everywhere, but after a couple of days we were sure he had met an untimely end. Having asked all the neighbors to check in sheds and garages, putting up notices all around the village and neighboring roads, we were sure that was the last we would see of our beloved boy. As a "just in case" measure, I would sleep with my window open, knowing that Saffi was safely shut in with my Mum.

One night, I was asleep and was suddenly aware of a cat rubbing my face. I thought it was Saffi and rushed to close my window so she couldn't get out, too. The absolute joy of seeing that it was, in fact, Silver was indescribable. I shouted to my Mum and sister, "He's back!" and we were all up, cuddling him and crying with relief. To celebrate his return, I immediately (at 2:00 A.M.) went into the kitchen to cook his favorite meal!

Sometimes the getaway might be naughty, but the return is glorious. Nothing makes the heart grow fonder than absence and worry.

Arthur

by Dory Bartell

Arthur is a chocolate and chestnut classic tabby. We got him at a cat show in the spring of 1991. Apparently his nose is too large for show quality. We took him to the vet only to find that he had ringworm, a virus, and a hernia. We had already fallen in love with him, so we could not send him back. He passed the virus and ringworm on to our other two cats, but after two months we got it all cleared up. Brave boy, he was altered and had his hernia repaired in the same day. He is a sweet lap cat, greeting everyone who comes to the house and sharing his chair. Arthur is thirteen now, but still full of life, enjoying the friendship of both of my Labs, though he weighs thirteen pounds and the dogs weigh seventy-eight pounds each.

Both dogs have their own beds, but Arthur presumes the beds are free space for him to cuddle. He rubs against the dogs and lets them drink out of his dish. If they go outside, he must follow on the porch. Although we have two other cats in the house, Arthur prefers the dogs. If I look for one, the other is always close by—I am beginning to suspect that Arthur may think he is a dog himself.

Not only is he a good friend, but he's there at my head in bed every night with his purring motor on all the time. As I am blind, it is particularly special to have all of these warm, furry animals in the house. All they ask for is a little love and good care, but they give so much more back. They're the best therapy anyone could desire.

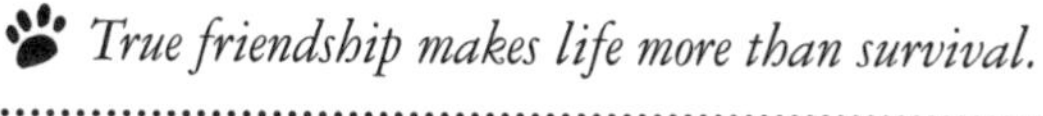
True friendship makes life more than survival.

The Enemy

by Diane Bell (a.k.a. Diabella)

Tropicana joined us at the age of ten months after being rescued from the roof of a six-story building. Life has not been the same since he arrived. I'll let him speak for himself:

Welcome! I'm a naughty kitty with big paws that have helped me destroy many things around here. Today, I beat up three vintage cookie jars and killed them by pushing them off the refrigerator in one shot! When I'm not busy looking for things to break or fight with, I enjoy shredding paper into confetti, or jumping on Diabella and the other cats and hitting them.

There are all kinds of things to attack around here, but I only have one real enemy. She's that fat lady with a silly grin who always sits on the kitchen counter. She's shiny and slippery. I yell at her and hit her often. I can't figure out why she never hits me back with that rolling pin. One good thing is that even though my food is right under the counter, she never eats any of it. Still, she is my enemy and I don't like her. Every time I turn my back on her, I feel her laughing at me. I'd like to drag her straight to my litter box and bury her.

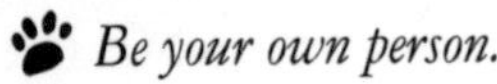

Be your own person.

Previously published on this writer's Web site (*http://diabellalovescats.com/trop.htm*) and condensed for this book.

Playing Submarines

by Lyn McConchi

There are a number of reasons why Tiger, my Ocicat, is excluded when I'm in the bath. My bath is one of the deep old-fashioned enamel-over-cast-iron types with the lion feet. I like the water pretty high—about two inches from the rim of the bath.

Last night, Tiger managed to sneak in and hide before I bolted the door, thinking he was on the other side. I climbed into all that lovely hot water and laid back, head on the rim and the rest of me semi-floating. Tiger then appeared. He beamed and hopped up to check the situation. Hmmmm. I was an island.

If he stepped down, he could sit on me and stay dry. He leaned over and planted his front feet. He was wrong about that because with the extra weight, I sank lower. The water crept up to his feet. He removed them. I rose. He stepped back. I sank, and he hastily took his paws back. Fascinated by this phenomenon, Tiger spent the next ten minutes stepping on and off of me while I went up and down like a submarine practicing crash dives.

It was NOT a peaceful bath. At last I gave up, washed hastily, and exited the water, Tiger at my heels in case I did something else interesting.

 *Determination and perseverance will help you accomplish your goals.*

Gertrude and Morris

by Elli Matlin

Gertrude appeared on August 23, 1971. I remember the date because Mom and I had just returned from the hospital where my niece, Beth, was born. We pulled into the driveway, and there under the overhang from the kitchen windows was a scraggly gray cat with three newborn kittens. Mom gathered them up, and amazingly, Gertrude allowed us, total strangers, to pick up herself and her kittens. We moved them into an indoor/outdoor kennel. We didn't have to worry about the dogs because they actually lived in the house. We placed two kittens into good homes and kept the last, Morris, for almost twenty years. Gertrude disappeared the minute her kittens were weaned.

Morris always lived with us, but he became my niece's cat, as they shared the same birthday. She had regular visiting rights. Although neutered, Morris became boss of the neighborhood and regularly got into battle. He was smart enough to fight only in our driveway or backyard so that whenever we heard cats fighting, we'd send out a dog to break it up. Morris would scrunch down on the ground, and the other cat, seeing a German shepherd coming, would take off. Of course, the dog chased the cat, but the cats always made it out the gate or over the fence and never got caught. Morris would then stroll into the house between the legs of the dogs.

How wonderful it is to feel protected and secure!

Now You See Them, Now You Don't

by Rod Marsden

A certain amateur magician had a great big top hat—a beautiful black stovepipe that was ideal for the pulling out of rabbits, an act that was part of the annual school festival.

Besides rabbits, this Hey! Presto! Guy and his family had Phyllis, a lady cat, and Trevor, a gentleman feline. Before long, Phyllis got pregnant, and three days before the festival, she pulled her own vanishing act. The family was frantic, but she was gone.

Showtime came, and with a heavy heart, Mr. Abracadabra climbed onto the stage. He was about to apologize for not being able to pull his rabbits out of the hat—they had refused to get in—when he felt something small and furry. He pulled it out and there was a squinting newborn kitten. He returned the tiny creature and pulled out another. The first one was a dusty gray like its mother and the second was a regal black like its father. All in all, he pulled six kittens out of his hat, and when he looked inside, there was Phyllis all curled up, happily feeding her babies, probably wishing her owner would stop messing with them.

From then on, Mr. Magician's yearly act was anticipated even more eagerly by the children. Would it be a kitten or a rabbit to come out this year? Phyllis knows he'd tell them if he knew, and her lips are sealed.

Life is full of surprises, and usually this is reason enough to stay positive during stressful times. Good things are right around the corner!

Kiki, the Cat of Many Names

by John R. "Jack" Vinson

My wife was leaving the doctor's office, and while unlocking her car, she heard a tiny "meow" behind her coming from under a bush. There she found a small shorthaired red tabby looking up at her and asking for something to eat. She brought him home and fed him, and that little cat ate for two days without taking a breath. During his first trip to the vet, they asked for his name to put on his records. I thought for a second and said, "Rusty," borrowed from one of my sister's cats.

Some time later, a friend wanted a cat, so we gave her Rusty. Her husband renamed him Buddy because he liked his companionship. Soon, however, Buddy started getting sick, and our friend said she couldn't handle a sick cat. It turned out that Buddy had been eating her houseplants, but we couldn't convince her of that. She called to say that Buddy was at the vet again, and she just wasn't going to bring him home anymore. He'd have to go to the ASPCA shelter. On hearing that, I went to the vet, paid his bill, and brought him back home where he belonged.

We finally ended up calling him—Rusty/Buddy—Kiki, which I think was short for kitty kitty. Kiki is smart. He can open the kitchen door any time he wants to, so now I need to teach him to close the door behind him. Come winter, he might open the garage door and let all the heat out.

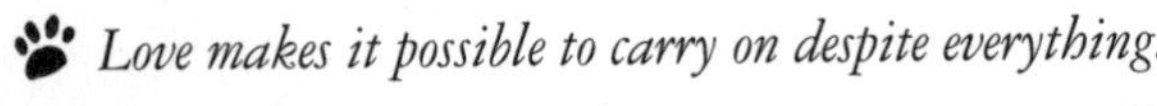

Love makes it possible to carry on despite everything.

Personal Trainer

by Theresa Mancuso

Well, I couldn't afford a personal trainer even if I were so inclined, but my cats are better than a trainer. I'm concerned about osteoporosis, so with as much regularity as I can muster, I get the old "bod" moving through an exercise routine, my favorite part—and my cats' favorite—of which is weight training.

Down I go to the mat, after speedwalking and then all but killing myself on the bike. I've had enough of stretching, pulling, and pushing all my moving parts. I pick up my weights and lift them overhead and out to the side, and then it happens. Midway through the weights routine, my personal trainer appears: any one of the cats in charge of my life. Leaping on my chest while I lie prone, he grabs the weights as I lift them upwards. If only he can get a free ride, he thinks. I pause between drills, and he marches down my body to sit atop my ankles when it's their turn for weight-bearing work. My best personal trainer is Marmaduke Rodgers, whose chirping voice keeps the count and forces me to the next level of difficulty. Without him, I'd probably lose heart one day and just become a couch potato, but with him, I'm a tiger ready to spring.

Taking care of yourself is important at every stage in life.

Miss Kitty, the Brave

by Rose Hosp

I visited a friend to help her set up her computer. When I arrived, I didn't spot her cats so I asked where they were.

"Oh, they're hiding," she said. "Seems they hide, and stay in hiding, any time someone comes to visit."

She signaled me to follow her down the hallway to the bedroom at the far end of the house. She indicated that the cats were in there. I peeked in, checking the windowsill, chairs, and dressers, but saw no cats.

Then, I saw it. At the far end of the foot of the bed—a slight bump in the bedspread! Yes, Miss Kitty gets up under the spread and stays there until all visitors leave. George, on the other end, simply sleeps under the bed.

As an aid to overcoming shyness, try to concentrate on helping others feel welcome and at ease.

6

Ferals, Shelter Cats, and Purebred Felines

Virtues to Live By

Life can be a challenge or a piece of cake. How we face whatever happens depends upon the qualities of the inner self: namely, virtues and characteristics of mind and heart. That's where inner strength comes from.

Ferals, shelter cats, pets, and purebred felines are in it with us. Compelled to survive by their own wits, they have uncanny supplies of courage and fortitude and determination to get on with it no matter what. Cats encounter troubles just like we do. They are amazing in their ability to survive, with a serenity that we'd do well to emulate.

In all of life's choices, the ones we like and the ones that are thrust upon us, our inner qualities (virtues) make all the difference in the world. Strive for wisdom, generosity, fairness, compassion, kindness, love, truthfulness, honor, fortitude, perseverance, and honesty. Money and fame do not solve the riddle of existence, but goodness makes sense of it all, and believe it or not, cats have something to teach us. They're cool, and we'll be cool, too, by walking the path of virtue.

Toffee's Tale

by Margaret Ambler

One day I got a phone call from a large farm ten miles away. The farmer was worried about the wild cats that ran around his property and asked me to help. Off I went, my car full to the brim with cat traps. I thought this would all be done in a day.

He showed me the largest barn I have ever seen, a barn the size of four normal ones. There I found more cats and kittens than you can imagine!

The job took three weeks of catching cats and kittens every day. I lost count after sixty. Many were ill. On the last day I got my eye on this cat disappearing down a small hole at the back of the barn. I had to make sure there were no kittens there. To my horror I found four dead kittens, and then, suddenly, I heard a small meow from the back of the hole. At the very bottom I found a tiny cream-colored kitten that was about five weeks old, soaking wet, and covered with lice and fleas. But he was alive. To my surprise, he purred when I came near, so I brought him home, cleaned him up, removed the lice and fleas, and straightaway, I named him Toffee.

I guess he was so glad to be warm and dry that he didn't mind my touching him, unlike most feral cats and kittens. Toffee is four years old now, a very happy fat cat!

The will to live is our greatest resource.

Ziggy

by Autumn sie Wolf

I was sitting at my computer and felt an intense headache coming on. I am not prone to these, but between my itchy skin cancer and my efforts to give up coffee, I decided to just take a break and sit with my eyes shut for a few minutes.

Our one-and-a-half-year-old Snowshoe cat, Ziggy, was asleep on the bed. As soon as I sat down, he got up and jumped to my lap. That was the first amazing thing because this cat is very partial to my husband and rarely comes to me. He continued to amaze me by insisting on getting right up on my chest and touching my *face*! Yes, he pressed his soft, warm belly right over my face and then proceeded to wash my face. The whole operation lasted about five minutes, but it seemed more like ten, and when he finally moved down from my face to my lap, *the headache was completely gone.*

Ziggy is not a lap cat, even for my husband, and certainly does not tolerate a belly rub. Nevertheless, Ziggy rose to the occasion, and after receiving his feline massage, I felt enormously better and thoroughly amazed.

I know that Ziggy understood. Hearkening back to the day I acquired him from a friend who found him as a stray kitten, the moment she handed Ziggy to me, I knew that I had something special: a sweet cat who can cure headaches better than ibuprofen!

Comfort the suffering; soothe the sorrowful; go where you are needed.

The Cat with Cartoon Book Eyes

by Theresa Mancuso

Why or how anyone in their right mind and proper conscience would dump a cat is beyond my comprehension. Truth be told, I have little mercy toward those who harm the harmless. Walking Abby, I often pass a corner house surrounded by a white picket fence and plenty of boulders, flowers, and fallen tree limbs that create a veritable paradise of hiding places for feral cats or one-time pets abandoned to the "wild." When first I met the cat with cartoon book eyes, it was by his invitation, not mine. He calmly approached Abby, who was already peeping through the white fence. They soon were nose to nose while I watched in amazement.

Presuming that the beautiful gray cat with enormous luminous green and turquoise eyes was someone's pet taking a walk outdoors, I put my hand over the fence. *Hisssssss!* came his reply, and up went a fluffed-out back, humped into a round tall monster with his tail lifted high and flicking right to left. *Hissss!* Withdrawing, I spoke to him gently; then Abby and I went on our way.

My feral-feeding friend, Lois, explained that the green-and-turquoise-eyed boy was undoubtedly an abandoned feline left to fend for himself. She named him Smokey and included him morning and evening in her feeding program. Smokey, at least, would be well fed along with Ms. Frick and Ms. Frack, the East Fifth ferals.

Smokey's beautiful eyes continue to appear through the underbrush as Abby and I round the corner early every morning. They follow us and, sometimes, Smokey comes closer to look us up and down, but so far, the cat with cartoon book eyes evades apprehension. Perhaps another day will prove successful.

Abandonment of pets is a despicable act of human selfishness and cruelty. Never dump a furry friend.

The Unexpected Hero

by Tina Juul

Quite a long time ago, shortly after my family moved into the house I would grow up in, there lived an ordinary kitten. The house was set back in the woods, and because all of my mother's other cats were purebreds and constantly in heat, they were kept indoors. But this one was a plain alley cat and therefore enjoyed the pleasures of roaming freely outside. She never went very far, as there were enough trees in the backyard to entertain her for hours.

One day, this little kitten managed to climb up an embarrassingly low-sitting crabapple tree and (being an inexperienced feline) just could not figure how to get down again. My mother, the ever hands-off maternal figure, simply watched from the kitchen window to see if this frightened tabby could find her own way out of the predicament she had gotten herself into. As she watched this helpless kitten mew pathetically for salvation, she also noticed the neighbor's orange tomcat racing up the hill toward the tree. He stopped, assessed the situation six feet above the ground, and leapt up to the first branch. In two seconds, he had reached the kitten and, as gingerly as a new mother cat, took her in his jaws and climbed back down to sturdy safety.

To this day, I don't remember what happened to that kitten in the end, but one thing is for sure: From that day on, that very ordinary kitten had a quite extraordinary friend for life.

Never underestimate your own unexpected heroic potential. Courage is often born because of circumstances.

Cat-Alog

by Caroline McRae-Madigan

A friend of mine owned a small country restaurant. I was visiting when she got an early morning call that she had to leave for a few hours. Then her staff called in sick! I put a "closed kitchen" sign in the window but opened the coffee shop (I had been there enough to think I could do that). It was very early in the morning when doors chimed, announcing the arrival of a customer. A man's voice inquired, "Is your catalog in?"

I turned a blank look at him and said, "Pardon me?"

He repeated, "Is your catalog in?"

I looked around and replied, "I don't think so, but we have yesterday's newspaper."

He looked at me very strangely and said, "Pardon?"

I responded, "Did you not just ask me if we had a catalog in?"

The man laughed and said, "No! I asked if your cat was allowed in!"

Apparently, there was a stray cat outside on the step when he came to the restaurant. My friend explained later that Millie was an old barn cat to whom she gave scraps every morning. From that day on, I cannot hear the word catalog without thinking about Millie!

Cultivate a generous spirit.

Courtesy and Respect

by Theresa Mancuso

I asked the noted animal communicator Marlene Sandler to help Primo and Marmaduke establish boundaries, overcome their sibling rivalry, and reduce hostilities, if she could. Marlene assured me that while we could not insist that the boys be happy together, we could demand courtesy and respect—and we did. My home became much more peaceful.

When Charlie joined the family, Marmaduke redirected his efforts. Instead of tormenting aristocat Primo, Marmaduke focused on helping Charlie adjust to his new home. Then one day all hell broke loose. I was busily at work on this very manuscript when I heard the mother of all hisses break forth as my furry beasts skirmished nearby. With avid determination, they leaped and flew at each other, Primo ever-striving for the high ground of defense, while Marmaduke thrust upwards with swatting tiger arms and no mercy.

My pleas brought no relief. Then I remembered. Going straight to the cupboard, I took out a can of Fancy Feast and scooped out large portions onto a big plate, singing a merry tune created for just this occasion: "Courtesy and respect, we eat and play together. Courtesy and respect, we eat and play together."

I kid you not. The boys were quiet for a few hours, cuddled together atop the counter, overfed and content!

Food isn't love, but its judicious application can work many wonders.

Schmeckel

by Barbara H. Vinson

About eight years ago, my friend Judy found Schmeckel in Brooklyn—or rather, he found her. She was outdoors enjoying a hamburger, when up came a little tuxedo kitten, demanding a piece. The kindhearted Judy gave him some, which he gobbled down in no time flat. Who knew when the little fellow had eaten last? Judy took the kitten home and then put him up for adoption. Of course, guess who came along and decided that he would make a good playmate for Zeppie?

Unfortunately, Schmeckel was feral and didn't trust humans, including me, but he did indeed make a wonderful playmate for Zeppie. As the years passed, Schmeckel has grown accustomed to me, but to this day I can't really handle him.

The pet psychic Sonya Fitzpatrick says that if you want a cat to do something, explain to him telepathically what it is that he needs to do and why. I tried this with Schmeckel one day in order to get him into a carrier to visit the vet. To my astonishment, into the carrier Schmeckel quietly walked!

So, it's perfectly possible to live with a feral cat, if you are willing to accept him on his terms. Schmeckel is content, and that makes me very happy. Besides, he's really rather cute with that slightly suspicious-looking expression on his face and his crooked little bowtie.

A little bit of kindness goes a long way.

The Runt

by Jackie S. Brooks

Timmy was an unwanted feral cat. We had adopted Sassie from the Cat League three weeks earlier, when I received a letter asking if we would take in a male kitten with big problems and try to make him people friendly! Hah. They know a sucker when they see one! After hours of trying to capture him, the lady brought him to us in a wire cage. He was terrified and was wailing so loudly, I think the whole village heard him.

Timmy was classified a "runt." (I HATE that word.) He was tiny, all skin and bone, and his tail seemed permanently glued to his tummy. He had been badly mistreated and was totally traumatized. He somehow managed to escape through the cat flap that night, though he barely had the strength to push it, and he was not able to get back in. The next morning, Jim found him wailing on the doorstep, wanting to come back in again.

Eventually, he allowed me to pick him up. I gave him pep talks as I tried to reassure and cuddle this poor little ginger scrap. I told him he was going to grow up to be a beautiful, healthy, strong, and muscular cat. His tail slowly became unglued, at first just following him limply, and then it started to rise up proudly.

That was nine years ago, and although he still has flashbacks that make him nervous, he is now the beautiful, healthy, strong, and muscular cat that I promised him he would be.

Heroism comes in all shapes and sizes.

Sunny and Shadow

by Fran Nickerson

Nearly forty years ago, long before cats were routinely spayed or neutered, there lived a small seal point Siamese female and a handsome natural mink Tonkinese male. Sunny was young, perhaps a teenager in cat years, and Shadow was her beau. Sunny became pregnant. When it was time for kittens to be born, she littered the house: the first kitten in the living room, another in the hallway, and the other two under our bed. We collected them and brought them to her, and she became a good mom. Shadow also cared for the kittens and would bathe them if Sunny left them alone. When the kittens were eight weeks old, we found good homes for them. The kittens were all picked up the same day. Sunny cried for her babies, and we felt terrible.

Shadow went outside. He caught a mouse and promptly brought it to Sunny. He had never before brought a mouse into the house, and never did again. He felt her pain and did what he could to help. Sunny clearly appreciated his gesture (though I removed the mouse quickly). There are times we all need to feel the love and caring Shadow gave Sunny.

🐾 *Every act of compassion makes the world a better place.*

7

Cats That Own Their People

Unconditional Love and Responsibility

An anonymous saying goes: "Thousands of years ago, cats were worshipped as gods. Cats have never forgotten this." We often joke that cats own the people who have them. The behavior that prompts these judgments is actually a manifestation of unconditional interspecies love between felines and their humans—and it's a great thing (though occasionally somewhat inconvenient). When you love, you must be responsible. True love does not exist without genuine responsibility, and the exercise of that responsibility is sweetened by the depth of love. Why else would anyone take care of another living being?

Unconditional love is generous, protective, understanding, forgiving, forbearing, and compassionate. It reaches beyond the moment, beyond appearances, mistakes, circumstances, and difficulties with a commitment that embraces the essence of the beloved in uncompromising fidelity. When you love someone unconditionally, you are ready to die for that person. Jesus said, "Greater love than this no man has, than to lay down his life for his friend."

I suppose the cats that have been heroes, rescuing their kittens and their people in disasters, have the most to teach us about unconditional love and responsibility. But even the ordinary, everyday kitty has something to say. Do cats own their people? Whatever the answer is, unconditional love and responsibility underpin the human-pet relationship.

Night Duty

by Anne Fawcett

Night shift at the vet clinic was a lonely business until I started sleeping with my patients. Who could resist? I'd do my hourly rounds, top up fluids, change litter trays, and my heart would inevitably melt at the sight of a kitten, pawing at me through the cage door.

The head vet told me, with a wink, never to let their pleading get to me, but I always caved. I was a wasted hot water bottle without them, but that wasn't the whole truth. I needed them as much as they needed me. These little strays curled up beside me as if they'd been there forever. They followed me on late rounds poking around the other cages as if to say, "Look at me!" The next morning I'd return them to their cages, and usually they'd have a new home by lunchtime.

Then I met Mike. A client had found her trying to cross the main road. Mike was a bold four-month-old kitten, and after a night sleeping tangled in my hair, she made up her mind to adopt me. There was no returning this kitten to the cage. She utterly refused to let me near her until I'd succumbed to keeping her.

Why was this female kitty named Mike? Before I gave her a name, she wouldn't come near me. So, from a distance, I thought Mike was a boy. By the time I realized my mistake, and Mike was satisfied that she wasn't leaving for anyone, the name had stuck.

Some things seem to be meant to be; we can neither understand them nor change them.

"Don't Call Me 'Penguin'"

by Theresa Mancuso

Coming up on his first birthday this autumn, Charlie has become quite the man, outgrowing his red tiger buddy by many inches. He towers above Marmaduke, whereas earlier, Marmie seemed a giant next to Charles. My animals are avid eaters. They come running from all directions whenever I open the refrigerator door, a cupboard, or a can. They pounce into grocery bags in their quest for edibles, and nothing goes into my mouth unless they have thoroughly examined whatever it is and asked for a share of their own. It's my fault, I suppose, for raising them with indulgence, but the result has been super-healthy pets that fear nothing and thrive on their voracious appetites.

So no one was surprised when the Ocean Parkway waif began to grow, but as he sprouted, it seemed like lead and iron were thickening his muscles without adding fat. He gathered several pounds of weight as his body stretched up and down, front and back. He seemed quite earnestly in pursuit of height and power, a climbing, leaping, inquisitive, everywhere-at-once ambassador of curiosity and goodwill. After several visits to the Brooklyn aquarium to view the penguins, I realized Charlie's stunning black-and-white coat shone as if polished, and he looked like a four-legged penguin to me.

I'm not much of a *Batman* fan, but I really enjoyed Danny DeVito's performance as the misshapen elfin crook that much resembled a penguin. Why not call Charles Andrew Shen "Penguin"! He looks like one! For a long time, he bitterly refused to answer me—he looked me in the eye, turned his back, and flicked his tail, demanding respect. *Charles Andrew Shen, if you please.*

He wouldn't have it any other way now, but oh, he fretted when his elegant handle was exchanged for a cold climate bird, he who so loves to snuggle in the warmth of Abby's German shepherd coat.

There is power in names. Be careful what you call yourself and others!

Vitamin Therapy

by Rose Hosp

While regaling us with stories about his new cat, my son told us about Marilyn's "vitamin." It seems that whenever he and his wife take their vitamins, there's a treat for Marilyn, who's right on the spot at the sound of the pills rolling out from the bottle. I take vitamins, too, so when my "grandcat" came to visit, ever the attentive grandma, I had some Marilyn treats on hand.

The first couple of days, I was as quiet as could be getting my vitamins and no Marilyn. However, by the third day, quiet or not, she was right there begging for her vitamin. During the rest of the visit, I had only to walk to that cupboard and Marilyn was there ready, just in case. It is, indeed, "the age of vitamin therapy," and thus we survived the week, my "grandcat" and I.

It is the love of family and friends that makes life infinitely worthwhile.

Fuji, the Siamese Cowgirl

by Donna M. Ramsay

Fuji was a fullbred Siamese cat, very mild-mannered and lovable. With her gorgeous blue eyes, overseeing all she considered her family, including our dogs, she would watch over her world faithfully as if on guard duty.

On a warm spring day, Fuji was lounging in the living room when a neighbor's dog came through the front door wanting to say hi and play. This was a new dog to the neighborhood, and Fuji took exception to his entrance into her world. In the blink of an eye, she bounded across the room and leaped on his back, her claws digging in as she rode him like a broncobuster. The neighbor's dog yelped, twisting and turning, as he tried in vain to get loose of her grip and shake her off his back.

Fuji steered him home, delivering him to his owners. Then, just as casual, as if she were merely making a neighborly call, she jumped from his back, lifted her nose up in the air, and strutted home. She seemed to realize that she had made it known thoroughly to the new neighbors and their dog that no one was to enter her world unless invited.

Personal and familial responsibility requires you to defend what is yours. Protect your home and family, for that is your right and duty.

Cassanova Faces Destiny

by Brenda Colbourne

Two months after one of his many operations, Cassanova developed a sinus infection that didn't respond to antibiotics. Further investigation revealed that he had developed a small hole in his palate, so he had a second operation. That, too, failed, and operation number three also failed to close the hole in his palate. On we went to operation number four. Another dismal failure!

There were many times when I thought the hour had come to call it quits, and this was one of them. It was four months since I had brought Cassanova home, and at no time had he complained about any of his treatment. Maybe he should have another chance.

So I decided to consult a specialist in small animal surgery. Fortunately, she thought the hole was repairable and booked Cassanova for his fifth operation. The expected cost of this operation was just over $700! Time and again people put their hands into their wallets and donated money toward his surgery expenses as Cassanova faced his fate. Without them, he would not have made it through all of his surgeries, and neither would my bank account!

Love finds a way.

Marmaduke Rodgers, Water Inspector

by Theresa Mancuso

Marmaduke Rodgers marches into every task, but none so persistently as chores at the kitchen sink or in the bathroom. Marmaduke is a dolphin dressed up in a cat suit, the veritable water inspector that keeps us safe from terrorist attack at reservoirs or water resorts where people depend on aqua fresca for refreshment and recreation. When I shower, Marmaduke Rodgers sits on the windowsill inside the shower—forget it if he gets wet. That's his duty. When I brush my teeth, Dentist Rodgers perches on the side of the bathroom sink.

Marmaduke seems worried lest any water anywhere in this apartment should ever pass without his inspection. He is honor bound to watch every single droplet in the system. Occasionally, though very rarely, just to keep me from believing my water purification system is foolproof, Marmaduke waits for me to turn my back. Then he washes two kitty paws in the pitcher of water that has come through the PUR® device on its way to BRITA® filtration. He chirps cordially as I turn around. Now, I ask you, is there something wrong with this picture?

Do your best to do your duty at all times.

Perlita Owns Pat

by Pat Ramirez

I adopted a petite seal point Siamese cat from a local rescue organization. A plea had gone out from the organization for a quick adoption because she was quickly going downhill. It was no wonder that this little girl was terrified, sick, depressed, and not eating. She had undergone a long journey all the way from Bolivia, through Miami, to her final destination: a shelter in Locust Dale, Virginia.

Little Perla came home with me. We were told she came from a home with thirty-three cats. Now she was alone and in a new home, isolated in my bedroom with a person who didn't speak her language. I spent the next month running back and forth to the vet and trying to coax her to eat. I brushed off my high school Spanish and tried everything to comfort the trembling little meezer.

Sharing pictures with colleagues, one comment made me stop and wonder if I had gone over the edge. Looking at a photograph of Perlita sitting on the clean white eyelet sheets on my bed before a plate of food, a colleague said in utter disbelief, "You feed your cat in your bed?"

I would have fed her wherever I could get her to eat and still do. Her companionship is worth more to me than the price of a set of sheets.

Nothing is too much for those we love.

How Do You Know If Your Cat Owns You?

Lorraine Williams

I have taken to following my cat, StarGirl, with my camera. "Give us a lovely pose now, baby," I sing out. "Look to the right. No, the right! OK, left's fine. Stay by that tree; you look adorable. I said stay-by-the-tree. Oh, well . . . The tree by itself will look artistic in the photo album, I guess."

Throughout the time that StarGirl and I have been together, I must've taken a thousand photographs of her. Probably five have been great. Of the others, you can only see her backside, or a blur, or the sofa where she'd been sitting one second before I clicked the camera.

I drag out her photos to show people. "And this is StarGirl," I say, "racing toward her food bowl."

"Where? Oh, you mean that splotch?" says George.

"And here she is," I continue happily, "getting closer to her food bowl. Here she's starting to eat from her food bowl. In this one, she's well into eating from her food bowl..."

"STOP! I can't take it anymore," George shouts.

"Oh, hang on, wait," I say. "She's just come into the room." I reach for my camera.

George sighs. He says, "You're addicted to that cat."

I ignore him. "StarGirl, honey," I coo. "Look over to Mummy. No, don't run away . . ."

I'm not addicted to StarGirl. No way. I just have a normal healthy interest in photography!

Never attempt to deny the obvious.

Sunny, the Sundance Kid

by Barbara H. Vinson

Sunny is a real character. I call him "the redhead." He's a red tabby who has a pair of the most gorgeous orange eyes I've ever seen. He can be "sunny" one moment and in a snit the next from not getting his way. He loves to tease the other cats (especially the girls) and then tries to sweet-talk his way back into their good graces. He considers himself the Household Head Honcho and struts around like he holds the mortgage on the place. (He probably wouldn't approve of my telling you that he's really a mush under all that machismo, and somewhat shy with strangers.)

Sunny originally belonged to a lady in New York who was very ill and had to give him up because she couldn't care for him anymore. So he ended up with a "cat collector" who had 160 cats! She was too busy "collecting" to provide adequate nutrition or proper veterinary care for the cats she had. Many of them were very ill.

Fortunately for the cats in that sad household, a friend of mine came to their rescue when the "collector" had to go to the hospital. I don't know how he did it, but he found homes or rescue organizations for every single one of those cats. I am still amazed at his having accomplished such a herculean task! Bless him!

Anyhow, that's how we got our redhead, who is now a big, handsome fellow. Love in red. Laugh in red.

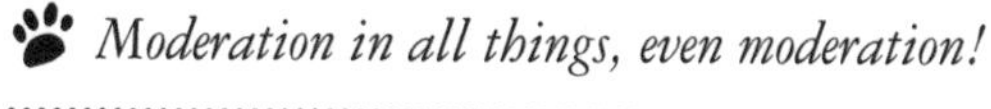

Moderation in all things, even moderation!

All Things Belong to Cats

by Theresa Mancuso

An English proverb says, "In a cat's eye, all things belong to cats." I have not a shred of doubt that this is true. Take this, for instance. My cats traverse our entire territory at will. They fly to the tops of bookcases. All of a sudden, I look up and there is a picture frame with Grandma's beautiful portrait tottering on the edge of the highest shelf, a self-confident kitty's paw ready to push it over. It falls to the floor. He grins, moves on to the next one. My car keys disappear from my desk and arrive at the counter or the dining room table, from which they plummet to the floor.

Feline marauders invade my pillow during the night, and there they sit, waiting for me to stir at the crack of dawn. The shower curtain is ripped. A cat (or several) has swung from it at will. One such master of all he surveys walked off with the very pen with which I was writing checks—and no apology, I might add.

I put my camera bag down on returning from a shoot. I turn around a moment later and see a silly cat sitting inside the bag beside my Canon Rebel. Red cats rule the world. So too, my friend, do grays, whites, blacks, browns, tabbies, and solids, felines of all descriptions. And I ask you, what would we ever do without them?

Unconditional love and forgiveness for cats is a taste of God's mercy that so surpasses our own.

Decibel and Mischief

by Linnette Horn

I have always been owned by felines, and currently I am food provider to Decibel and his nephew Mischief. Decibel is a gray tabby and white cat and Mischief is red tabby and white. They both have solid purrs and get into plenty of mischief. Decibel is a great tree climber. At the top of the climb, he will hang like a small limpet, then reverse and come roaring down his access route at high speed.

Mischief is famous in the neighborhood for getting himself locked into basements when he goes out mousing. For him to miss one meal is unusual, but to miss two is the signal for a Mischief alarm to be broadcast and neighbors to be put on alert.

Last winter, Mischief got himself locked in a basement after the neighbor went overseas. I had gone looking for him, as it was getting dark. I could hear the anxious meowing of a cat, and as I shone the light of the torch in the direction of the neighbor's basement windows, I was treated to the sight of one anxious little cat all but bouncing up and down on the bench inside in a frantic attempt to answer my calls. He was let out eventually, after a second neighbor helped me break in, whereupon he was greeted by us and a worried Decibel, who hissed at him for causing all the concern!

The fact that our kids and pets may be mischievous seems to add to our affection for them and enjoyment with them. They keep us young at heart.

The Milk Pot

by Peter P. Dachille, Jr.

Among the pots and pans in the kitchen there's a small saucepan. It doesn't match the others; the yellow and brown paint is scratched and there are a few dents, including one that threatens to open as a hole someday. We dare not throw it out, though; it is the "milk pot," which I guess symbolizes how spoiled Sam, our twelve-year-old tabby/Angora cat, is.

Yes, Sam gets his milk warmed up. These days we justify it, saying it makes him sleepy, but we've no actual proof that it has the same effect in felines as people, since cat sleeping patterns are constant! We don't dare take the pot out when Sam wanders into the kitchen, even to heat up some small amount of sauce or gravy, as the telltale color and shape mean only one thing to him: milk! Meowing quickly follows and will not end until a warm saucer of milk is before him.

Of course, it must also be the correct temperature, or he will walk away, a flick of his tail signaling disdain, until it cools down. If it is "purrfect," he'll dive his face in and lap away, then come to one of us, showing us the remnants of a milk mustache slowly disappearing. It's about as close to thanks as we get, but I'll take it!

We are all creatures of habit. Make sure the habits you acquire are good ones!

....

So Much for Heritage

by Lorraine Williams

It all started when I had afternoon tea at my friend Ramona's place. Ramona bellowed at her cat, "Muffin! Don't you dare be sick on the carpet!"

Muffin stopped in midretch. Her expression read, "Oops!" She fast-pawed it to her litter box.

Ruh-uh-hhhhhh-HA!

"Good girl, Muffin," said Ramona smugly.

I was in awe. "How'd you do that?" I asked. "Train her to be sick in her litter box?"

Ramona insisted it was all down to heritage: "After all, Muffin *is* Persian."

Heritage, eh? My cat, StarGirl the Siamese, oozed heritage. That night, I had a serious talk with her. "StarGirl, you're going to have to learn responsibility," I said. "I want you to be more like Muffin. Do you understand?"

StarGirl crossed her eyes at me, a sure sign she was cranking up to a mood. Her tail swished. *I spit on Muffin!* She hightailed it outside for a marathon grass-chewing session. I sighed. Soon, I guessed, there'd be another regurgitation patch on the carpet.

The next week Ramona rang me to sorrowfully reveal that Muffin had vomited again, this time on the lounge rug. So much for training and heritage.

StarGirl and I rejoiced in Muffin's downfall. StarGirl especially. There was now no paragon of virtue for me to hold up to her as a shining example of how she should conduct herself. StarGirl leapt up onto the sofa. *Me-ooww, come here and pat me*, she ordered.

"Coming," I said meekly. StarGirl has me trained to perfection.

It's a fact that most of us are willing to go to all sorts of extremes to please and satisfy the object of our affection.

8

Courageous, Faithful Felines

Make the Best of Things No Matter What Happens

My nephew was four years old when he said, "No matter what happens in life, you must never be angry with yourself. Just make the best of it." Most cats are delightful with youngsters, and most children love cats, and this kid did, too. But when I visited him one time and brought a couple of kittens from the shelter, he stood up tall and, with all the honesty of his little heart, mustered up his courage and said, "We don't want your kitties, Aunt Tree." If you put kids and cats together, you've got to watch them to keep it safe and copacetic. But once you get a cat to love a kid, you've got a mighty courageous and faithful feline at your service. Cats show courage and fidelity in many ways, and we can do the same by contemplating the cat.

Step back and watch the way a faithful feline lives. Notice the courage of ordinary everyday cats. They sure make the best of things without a lot of fuss. Go for the gold when the situation's not easy; muster up the courage and faith you need to keep a project alive when it seems doomed, if there's any chance at all to redeem it and if it's a worthy cause. There are lots of ways that courage and fidelity can help you make the best of things, and my life with cats has often brought that fact to the fore in the strangest of ways. Let there be no anger in your heart, and do not feel frustrated or bewildered at everything untoward that happens. Being honest, faithful, and courageous with yourself and others makes it possible to search through life's ungainly piles of puzzles and disenchantments to find a way to make the best of things no matter what happens.

Cassanova's Cage

by Brenda Colbourne

On a visit to one of the local animal shelters, I saw a forlorn-looking cat that was curled up in a basket at the bottom of the cage. The staff told me that when he ate, the food came out of his nose because he had a hole in the roof of his mouth. Not exactly the kind of information to inspire a potential adopter, but something made me go back a couple of days later to see what he was like. That was the start of my love affair with Cassanova.

He had a cleft palate, a broken leg, and an ulcerated left eye, and he also suffered from a sinus infection. Prior to my final decision to adopt Cassanova, I took him to a vet to obtain a quote for repairs. I received the first of many shocks. The vet said, "Up to $700!" Such a sum seemed unobtainable, and I thought, "That's that."

I spent a sleepless night wondering if I had made the right decision, and by morning, I decided to go ahead and rescue him, believing I would manage somehow as I always did before. Juggling finances to save Cassanova was a way of life, but well worth it because he is finally a happy, healthy kitty in a new home!

Make those tough decisions, grit your teeth, and keep on going. Things usually turn out for the best, but it often takes guts to make it happen.

A Killer in Denmark

by Tina Juul

Although it's a cat's instinct to hunt, we Americans sometimes deny our feline friends that pleasure because we want to protect our feathered friends against a slow and ghastly death.

Here in Denmark, where I live, people take sides with their beloved pets, with little consideration for the nearly defenseless birds. My cats are the only ones in the neighborhood that wear collars with bells and name tags. It's mostly for their protection, but I took the birds into consideration as well, making sure the bells were loud enough to warn them of their potential demise should they tarry where cats were lurking.

The neighbors are disconcerted that their cats are forced to wear this shameful stigma. As opposed to being concerned for the birds' welfare, they think it unfair that cats be made to don these jingling pendants, thus destroying any chance to make a "proper" kill, as they are programmed to do.

Dexter, being a proper cat, proved them wrong last summer by proudly making two kills from our tiny terrace. Sad to say, that cat let those little birds die those slow and ghastly deaths due to another natural instinct—play.

I, of course, discovered all of this hours after the birds had perished. Dexter only did what she knew to be right, acting according to her nature.

There's no fail-proof escape or complete deterrence from your own true nature. Learn to love yourself.

Zeppelin

by Barbara H. Vinson

It was a Saturday afternoon at one of Manhattan's busiest pet shops. Off in one corner sat Patty, who had several cats on exhibition in the hopes of finding them homes. She and her friends worked very diligently at this and were faithfully there every weekend, rain or shine. Sometimes, they would have a lucky day where several kitties were adopted; at other times, it was disappointing—not a one found a home.

On this particular Saturday, I happened to wander in and was immediately captivated by a tiny black-and-white kitten up for adoption. He couldn't have been more than four weeks old and looked *so* confused and frightened—a little speck of life in an oversized cage. My heart went out to him at once, and I made immediate arrangements with Patty to adopt him. The little fellow hadn't even been fully weaned, but he learned to eat practically overnight, he was so hungry. In fact, he ate so much that his little sides stuck out, making him look as if he could just float away—like a miniature zeppelin. Of course, Zeppelin became his name!

Zeppie has now grown into a handsome young tuxedo cat with perfect markings—black bowtie, collar, and cummerbund. He is so dapper that it's a pity he and Fred Astaire can't go out on the town.

Well, I reckon Zeppie will have to be satisfied with being all dressed up and no place to go!

To consistently make the best of things, no matter what's going on around you, tune in to your feelings, observe what your senses tell you, listen attentively to what your body says, and focus all of your inner being on the intuitive guidance that comes from within. Let it penetrate your conscious mind, trust it, and act upon it.

Banana Pancakes at Eva's

by Edy Makariw

It was a beautiful day. I woke up fidgety, crabby, and unfocused. My partner's mood seemed no better. Hoping that a change of scenery might do us good, we went out for breakfast together. We continued to interact in an antagonistic, nonproductive manner, and I suggested we just cease fire, let our meals arrive, and give our moods and our blood sugar levels a chance to improve.

We continued to glower at everything and nothing as we sat there in "time-out" mode, during which I overheard one of the coffee shop regulars at the table next to ours tell the waitress that he was looking for homes for a litter of young kittens that his dog had found in the neighbor's garage.

As my already more harmonious partner and I were heading out after eating, I gave the man my phone number and told him I'd be happy to take whatever kittens he hadn't placed by the following week, when I returned from a brief vacation. I'd be moving into the recently vacated top floor of our house, while my partner remained on the first floor. And what nicer housewarming present to myself than a new life (or two)?

Harmony with our destiny is built upon accepting the consequences of every decision and made easier by trusting that, at each step along the way, whatever happens to us is usually for a higher good.

Saving Missy

by Selma L. Wiener

I missed Ginger when he passed on; he had been a marvelous companion cat. The heart mends slowly sometimes.

Soon after Ginger's death, friends of mine who lived upstate happened upon a dreadful scene. They were driving on a highway when the car in front of them slowed down, came to a brief halt, and swatted a small kitten out the back door. There it was, alone and beleaguered by the cruelty of humans who did not want to keep it. My friends stopped and rescued the little waif from the roadside. They called me as soon as they were back in the city and asked me if I would like to adopt the small kitten that had been so harshly treated in its very young life. I agreed to take the little stranger and called her Missy. She took to me much faster than I took to her. We both had grief, but in her tiny kitty soul, Missy knew she had been saved. Together, we braved the first days in which I was hanging on to Ginger. But the days went by and she grew and grew. Today, Missy is a beautiful tabby cat, and we're best friends, two lone beings who have forged a friendship and home.

When loss comes into our lives, we aren't always capable of making the best of things by ourselves. Life is a good teacher, and consolation and comfort might come to us in surprising ways.

Lily Makes the Best of It

by Fran Pennock Shaw

Lily got by so well you'd hardly know she was blind in one eye—except that the eye was sewn shut, so you couldn't ignore the evidence. She still saw well enough to lick up every morsel in her food bowl. She still found her way to every favored spot—the sunlit bay window sill, the top of the refrigerator, and the hand-crocheted bedspread.

Outdoors was different, though. In the past, Lily had never turned down an opportunity for a breath of fresh air, although she wasn't crazy about donning the required halter and leash. In her backyard, she would sniff and snort through the high grass, often staring for five minutes at a single flower, pouncing on grasshoppers and other assorted bugs. A fairly good huntress, she tried to sneak her prey back into the house to play with. But now this part-Persian, part-tiger cat feared the outdoors. That worried her owner, who kept encouraging Lily (on her leash) to go out and smell the flowers.

Weeks passed. Finally, Lily reclaimed her adventuresome nature by chasing and clobbering a fall leaf, thinking it a butterfly. She trotted happily home with her "kill" clenched in her teeth. Then we all knew that glaucoma took Lily's eye but not her spirit.

Time and age will eventually get the better of our physical gifts and abilities. We must strive courageously to make the best of things. We are all crippled, but we all must learn to dance.

Ginger the Wild

by Elli Matlin

Ginger, our half-Persian, half–Maine coon cat, was very strange. Besides being huge, she had more wild traits than a Persian. She delighted in driving people crazy by climbing up into trees and hanging out on tree limbs. Just about when we would realize that there was a commotion outside because "the poor cat is stuck in the tree," Ginger would casually climb down from the tree, head first, as if nothing was going on around her. I really think Ginger enjoyed the whole thing, and we, though nerve-wracked at times, enjoyed her, too.

Ginger had a strange sense of humor. Lying on a tree branch at night, Ginger loved to drop down onto a passerby's shoulders, causing all sorts of hysteria. Then she'd leap off and walk away casually, as if nothing happened. To tell the truth, we would try to hide at that point and not claim ownership of the cat. Fortunately, those were simpler times, and we never got sued for shock or mental anguish caused by our cat's gingerly antics.

Ginger was never very good about coming when called, unlike our other cats. But Ginger loved liver, which my mother used to cut up with a large pair of scissors. When Ginger refused to come on call, we'd take the scissors outside to the front porch and snip them together, as though we were cutting something. She'd come running. Of course, we had to give her a reward for coming, so there was always a good supply of liver on hand.

To accept others for what they are, you must first accept yourself.

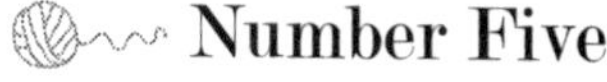

Number Five

by Karen Heist

The night we moved my sister to college, the weather was terrible, and I found a beautiful, soaking-wet cat rooting through garbage. "Hello, kitty!" I said. The surprised cat looked up with a tremendously long, loud meow: Help me; I'm hungry. I had no food then, but several hours later, the dog food arrived for my sister's guide dog, so we put down several mounds of it with water for the cat. Before leaving, I made my sister promise to feed the cat often.

A couple months later, my sister decided that the college was not prepared for blind students. She wanted to return home, so my parents went to help her. She had the cat in a carrier, ready to send it home for me, but on the way, somewhere in Delaware, my stepfather opened the cage to feed the cat and it got out and disappeared.

Devastated, I put an ad in the paper and posters everywhere. The weather turned bitter cold. Several attempts ended up in rescues for other cats, but not "mine." I was about to give up when someone called and left a message, but my return calls didn't connect. A cat that looked like "mine" was found dead on the street. We thought it was over.

Ten days before Christmas, I got a call, and I heard a plaintive meow over the phone. Someone had found my cat!

We call her Angel 007 even though "she" turned out to be male.

If your cause is right, persevere to the end, no matter what happens.

Feline Life Preserver—A Reason to Live

by Barbara Custer

Cathy gazed into the Delaware River's murky water. Howling wind nipped her cheeks, reminding her of the warning written by her boss, only days after her father's death and weeks after her husband walked.

Suddenly, she felt something soft rubbing her ankles. Looking down, Cathy found herself staring into the lime-green eyes of an emaciated Persian cat. Quivering on the curb, the cat gave her a pleading look. Crusty sores peeped through its soiled, tangled fur, the paws extended, whiskers long, ears up, and eyes desperate.

Cathy's trembling hand reached down to brush the cat's back. Her fingers felt protruding ribs. The cat needed a vet, someone she couldn't afford. Why not let it go? Perhaps it reminded her of a Persian she'd owned in high school before family circumstances had forced her into a foster home. Its sick appearance and weak mewing whispered a rumor of abandonment. In its dark pupils, she saw a lost expression, the same loneliness she'd seen forever in her own mirror. A lump rose in her throat.

"I can't let you die." Quickly, she scooped the cat into her arms. "Ladislav," she whispered, knuckling tears from her eyes. "Laddy for short; that's what they called my dad. I'll find a way around your vet bills."

She smiled, feeling love surge through her body. She was still facing an ill-tempered boss and ex-husband, but that didn't seem important now. Smiling again, she cradled Laddy against her chest and walked home in the twilight.

Having a sentient being to care for and nurture is the highest motivation for life.

9

Curious Cats

Stay Interested and Involved in Your Life

Upon entering new territory, cats explore every nook and cranny, even managing to climb into corners you forgot existed. They check out everything before they settle down. Feline ability to prowl and pounce is legendary. Cats often return to hide in dark places—in closets and under beds or chairs. Some cats hide from fear or shyness, but generally cats hide out just to observe the world at large. Cats are always alerted by and interested in new sounds, movements, and scents. Unthreatened, they will curiously scope out every new opportunity to explore their own territory and beyond.

Like the curious cats we love, we must also stay interested and involved with life. Never let yourself grow tired of living or bored with your surroundings. New ideas and new projects keep us forever young, creative, and alert. Stay involved and explore every opportunity to learn and do. Increase and stimulate intellectual curiosity by reading every single day. Step out of the ordinary to look beyond everyday experience. Travel, television, film, theater, work, and creative arts enhance life and help us to stay interested and involved.

 Ballerina

by Theresa Mancuso

My longest-living cat was a purebred Tonkinese named Nikki, who lived a long and happy life in the midst of my pack of German shepherd dogs, along with her Siamese buddy, Maximus. For over twelve years, I shared my Brooklyn home with three huge German shepherds and two cats, and the living was great. Nikki created numerous imaginative routines in order to gain center stage in our furry household. When guests visited, Nikki performed her full repertoire of kittenish delights, including intricate ballerina twists and turns, twirls, and poses much to the surprise of friends, many of whom began to refer to Nikki as "the ballerina." Whatever those antics may have meant in cat talk, the inevitable effect was to capture her audience completely and establish her role as the center of attention. Nikki was not a great talker, not in cat sounds, that is; but with quasi-mystical maneuvers, she outspoke everyone in the place, humans, canines, and other cats. Nikki held court twirling her beautiful lithesome body in coquettish pirouettes. Sometimes, though rarely, she even chirped in a soft voice, nearly inaudible.

When Nikki was satisfied that her place had been duly recognized, she gracefully left center stage and wrapped her lovely body seductively as a comfortable shawl about the shoulders of the most appealing human present, myself or a guest, depending on her fancy of the moment. Never shy, Nikki maintained ballerina prominence well into her older years and then quietly took her place on a satin pillow from which she observed all comings and goings.

If you're meant to be a great performer, let nothing hold you back, neither your own shyness nor the opinion of others. Wield your prowess and follow your dream.

Hide and Seek

by Gail Smart

As a child, did you ever play that game where you hide and someone hums as the seeker gets closer? My little Blob loves that game.

Blob is a curly-coated Devon Rex, just one year old and a total delight. Like any Devon Rex, he is very active and always climbs to the highest spot in any room. Kitchen wall cupboards are his favorites and the curtains are a must. However, in his rare quiet moments, he likes to hide himself away quite out of sight.

Unlike my vocal Orientals, who reply immediately if I speak or call them, Blob never replies. I become more and more frantic, searching the house for him. Blob loves people, and although he won't reply, he expects me to keep looking for him, and finally, to lift him down or out of his chosen spot. He keeps silent while I run around looking everywhere, but then he can't resist purring in anticipation of being "rescued."

As I get closer and closer, Blob starts to purr happily, purring louder and louder the closer I get to discovering him hidden under some blankets or behind a curtain. He actually turns his purr up as I get closer, and it fades quickly if I miss him and walk past. If Blob is under the blankets, I really can't understand how he knows exactly where I am, but he seems to be sure that I shall keep going until the rescue is complete.

Play is essential to physical, emotional, mental, psychological, and spiritual well-being.

A Tough Guy Faces the World

by Catherine Miller

Curly is even rough and tumble when he's being affectionate. He likes to rest the upper part of his body and forepaws on my lap. Many cats knead their owner's stomach or chest. Not Curly. He pushes at my stomach with his paws as one of us might fluff the pillows on a sofa, beating my abdomen into submission before he settles in. He gives body sculpting a whole new meaning.

One day, I thought I would expand his horizons and take him for a walk around the park that borders my house. It's a tree-lined, river-fronting Eden that always drives my heart rate down.

When I looked up after locking the front door behind me, Curly was nowhere to be found. All I could see was his leash extending from my hand to a spot underneath my car. When I finally pulled him out, he took one look around him, made a mad dash for the bushes, and peered out warily as though he were being stalked.

Covered by now in automotive grease and scratched by the bushes he had pulled me into, I soon realized that Curly preferred being a big cat in a small den than a small cat in a big one. It was ironic and a little sad. I was utterly convinced by his bravado from watching him at home, but the world I'd hoped to share with him outside the house was far too big for him to feel secure, much less in control.

Strive to expand your universe; open up your horizons and welcome new experiences.

Dopey and Sneezy

by Lyn McConchie

Now and again I look after a friend's Siamese kitten. Chang is a darling and he and Tiger get on very well. But there are times when I wonder. Tiger gets up to some rather weird things, but sometimes Chang is even odder.

I got back from a local auction at about 11:00 P.M. one Friday last month and parked my weary self on the bed to watch several TV programs that I had taped earlier. After a while, I became dimly aware that Chang was emitting little kitten sneezes, polite but vigorous. Not paying much attention to him, I finished watching TV, and then I realized that Chang was still sneezing madly and had been for ages. I rose to investigate; by now I was quite worried about the sneezing that had apparently never stopped. The cat sounded as if he was about to sneeze his nose completely loose.

To my bemusement, I found him sitting by the chest of drawers in the corner of the bedroom with his little black nose buried in the socks I had just taken off. He was continuing to sneeze vigorously. I removed the socks hastily, and the sneezing stopped at once. What baffles me still is, if they made him sneeze so much, why didn't he just take his nose out of them? Perhaps this is some sort of complicated and subtle cat insult?

Take care of your health; you're the one inside that body of yours!

Foil Fetching Tricks

by Tina Juul

When Dexter was a kitten, my sister taught her Ragdoll to fetch like a dog (as this was a special talent of the breed) and suggested that despite Dexter's alley cat status, I should try the same. I had no toys in the house, so I took a piece of foil and crunched it up into a ball, continuously chanting, "Where's the foil, Dexter? Where's the foil?" My high-pitched voice eventually had some effect on her as she perked up and waited impatiently for me to actually do something. I threw the foil, and she ran after it, swatted it around for a few minutes, and miraculously brought it back to me. We repeated this process for about an hour before she was finally hooked.

Now she will actually bring me the foil whenever she wants to play. She will find one of her dozens of foil balls under the couch and drop a good dusty one in my lap. As she is a "water cat," she will vary her playtime by rinsing the ball in her water dish first, then dropping it in my lap, nice and clean. And wet. Sometimes I come home from work to find the foil already soaking in the water dish.

This proves that although she knows I will always throw that slimy thing for her (she prepares for the hunt at the mere utterance of "where's the foil?"), she is the ultimate orphan, always able to amuse herself when no one else is around.

By word, manner, and enthusiasm, you can induce cooperation from the most reluctant companions, associates, or charges.

Story as Told by Pookah, a Gray Mackerel Tabby Neuter

by Pookah with Daphne R. Macpherson

One Saturday morning, a father and son drove into our driveway towing a small trailer with a little car in the back of it. While those people were talking to my people, I thought I'd investigate this strange-looking car, so I hopped aboard. I was in the little car when, to my horror and surprise, it started moving! After many hours of hiding in the little car, I was so cold, scared, and hungry that when it finally stopped, I was too tired to move.

The boy looked into the little car, found me, and took me inside their camper. For the next two days, I was treated as royalty deserves—the people fed me tasty tuna, chicken, even potato salad, and gave me a comfy pillow to sit on so I could look outside and watch the people race the little cars. People came to see me, the cat who traveled 200 miles from Seattle to Portland hiding in the little car. They petted me, gave me treats, and told me what a marvelous, brave, and intelligent cat I was!

I rode back home inside the people car in comfort on the back of the seat. When we got home, Mom and Dad were overjoyed to see me! They had been so worried—I guess next time I want to travel, I'll tell Mom and Dad where I'm going first!

True adventure is whatever thrills and delights you, captures your imagination, and fires up your enthusiasm for life. A spark of danger might be tantalizing as long as it's only a spark and not a conflagration. Be careful in your quest for adventure!

Shusha

by Jose Antonio Brito

When I first moved into my apartment in Washington Heights last year, the place seemed huge and empty, so I wanted a companion cat. With my work schedule, a cat would definitely be easier to take care of than a dog. Off I went to visit a local pet shop in my search.

As I walked in, I asked the clerk, "Do you have any cats?"

"Sure thing, buddy, they're all in the back."

I went back and saw about fifteen cats in one cage, every single one black. They looked so scraggly and forlorn that I said,

"No way. No black cat for me." But something inside nudged me, and I turned around to stare right into the little beady eyes of a black kitten that seemed to say, "Take me, take me . . ." I changed my mind and took her home.

Shusha's been the best thing for me, the sweetest cat to live with. When life's troubles hit and I feel bad about something, Shusha's happy look tells me everything will be OK. And it usually is.

For a long time after I brought her home, I was unable to hold Shusha or caress her for very long. She seemed to have a wild side. Then, one day, as Shusha lay beside me in bed, I was able to caress her, and she cuddled up snug against my side. At last, Shusha made up her mind to stay right next to Daddy.

Patience is the kindness we give to other living beings while we wait for what we want to happen. Everybody needs patience, both as receiver and giver.

....

Cat Alert

by Lyn McConchie

I was taking a long, hot bath one night when Tiger, hurling himself furiously at the door, managed to open it to join me. He puttered happily around, poking into boxes, the big wool bag, and other assorted containers stored at the back of the oversized room. One of the boxes was the original container for my word processor. I keep it so that if I need to send the machine for repair, I have a suitable box complete with polystyrene bits with which to pack the machine safely. Tiger discovered this interesting fact, and some time later, just as I was considering dislodging myself reluctantly from the loving embrace of vast amounts of hot water, he came wandering out to peer up at me.

I glanced back and gaped in horror. Tiger was foaming at the mouth! A second look and I realized that he was chewing a piece of the polystyrene. That was even more upsetting! If he ended up swallowing any of it, he would require the vet.

I scrambled, dripping from my bath, and persuaded Tiger to surrender his foam, and then I carefully folded the box shut, hoping he would find it more difficult to climb in and chew on things again. But that first glance did give me something of a shock. Envisioning some of the things that could happen if he swallowed it gave me far more: Imagination is a writer's curse.

Curiosity can get you into trouble. Mind your own business and you'll never have to fear that which kills cats—that is, some cats.

Computer Nerd and Clothes Rack Demon

by Elli Matlin

My rough-and-tumble cat, Islip, has a thing for my computer keyboard. Maybe he's a computer nerd at heart. Whenever I am on the computer, Islip has to walk across the keyboard. This, of course, creates havoc with my work, and Islip's intent seems particularly focused when the work at hand is important. Sometimes, as a result of Islip's attempts at computer literacy, weird letters appear in my work, but at other times, he manages to wipe out whole files.

Part of his problem is that Islip is utterly ungraceful. His large paws and heavy body traverse the keys like the rampage of an elephant through a field of peanuts. Islip's intentions may be pure. Perhaps he just wants a chance to be the world's greatest computer cat.

When I lived in Brooklyn, I had an old clothes rack for drying clothes down in the basement, standing against the staircase. Islip would go up the stairs and out between the uprights to stand on top of the clothes rack. Unfortunately, the clothes rack was not that sturdy, and when Islip pushed off the top to jump down, the clothes rack would inevitably fall and all my clean laundry would land on the floor. Only slightly surprised by the mishap, Islip's facial expression seemed to declare, "This is a cat's prerogative, after all!"

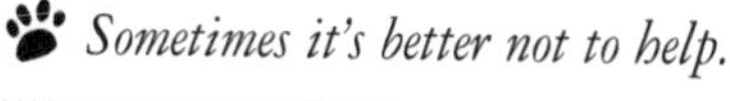

Sometimes it's better not to help.

Penelope's Worst Day

by Ed Kostro

She sat passively in her tiny cage at the big city animal shelter, sadly watching the other cats and kittens being played with, talked to, and adopted. No one gave her the time of day.

Penelope was eight years old, left to fend for herself in a downtown apartment, her callous former owner not caring one bit about her fate. The building superintendent found her, as he had found hundreds of her kind before—abandoned. Her hurriedly dumped her at a shelter so he could get back to his business for the day.

Although Penelope had been starving when she was found, she had no appetite this day. Mournfully, she gazed at the food dish beside her, and although she was very thirsty, she ignored the water bowl, too. Penelope could not understand what she had done wrong. She could not understand why no one loved her anymore. But she was wise. She knew in her broken heart that her future looked extremely grim.

Her sad eyes had already clouded over in resignation when I stopped in front of her. She barely noticed me gazing down at her. I opened her cage door and carefully lifted her into my arms. I gently stroked her long, regal fur. Her eyes slowly opened, her shattered heart began to mend, and she purred from the very depths of her feline soul. That evening in my home, Penelope enjoyed the best night of the worst day of her life.

Never abandon hope. Life is full of surprises, and your best one may be just around the corner.

....

More Kitten Antics

by Lillian Howell

We put our kittens to bed in the downstairs bathroom. Prince took it literally, and we found him in the toilet the next morning, too small to get out. That didn't stop him from exploring.

We had decided to put them there to allow our older cat, Blackie, access to the cat flap. But Prince devised his own cat flap. His great escape was to jump from toilet seat to sink to windowsill, stretch up to the top pane, which was usually ajar, and scramble out to leap the six feet to the ground. Then he'd come around back to show off what he could do.

I've never figured out why cats need to wake you at 5:00 A.M. to be let out when they could easily walk out through the unlocked cat flap! That's the whole idea of having one. Perhaps they want a night doorman. Besides meowing to get you out of bed, there's the paw pat to the nose that's very effective, or they bite your toes. You think of keeping the bedroom door shut, and they claw the carpet by the door. It's easier to just get up!

Try out new things; it will help you keep interested and involved in life when you feel ready to throw in the towel.

Losing Wellington

by Audrey Elias

When Wellington disappeared, after searching our building thoroughly, we concluded that our naive, indoor cat must've somehow gotten outside, onto the streets of Manhattan.

We reasoned that he'd be terrified by all the hubbub of the streets and would hide until late at night. So at 4:00 A.M. my husband, Mickey, went out to search. No Wellie. The next night was the same. We tried to resign ourselves to his loss.

Then on the third day, a realtor who'd been showing the vacant apartment above ours tapped on our door. "Did you lose a cat?" she asked. "I just saw one upstairs."

Mickey ran up. Indeed, there was Wellie's face, peering from a hole in the ceiling above a sleeping platform. He wasn't trapped, but fear had made him into a wild thing—even when I'd gone into that apartment and shaken treats and called, he didn't come to me. Now when Mickey went to lift him down, he struggled and scratched viciously. It was amazing what a transformation fear, dehydration, and hunger had wrought in him—fortunately, it was temporary.

A few years later, Wellie vanished again, this time from our house in Brooklyn. Again we were convinced he must've gotten outside. But after several days, we heard quiet mewing late at night, and it turned out that he'd "gone wild" again, hiding in garbage our upstairs tenants had piled on their landing, a pile we thought we'd inspected thoroughly.

Hunger, fatigue, fear, and other emotions can transform most people into unrecognizable "others." Safety and security are restorative.

Can Cats Dance?

by Diane Bell (a.k.a. Diabella)

Have you ever wondered what it would be like if cats could speak? Or dance? Have you ever wondered what your cats do after the lights go out? Have you ever given any thought as to how cats entertain themselves once they are certain that you are fast asleep?

I had the strangest dream last night. It all began with a veil of puffy pistachio clouds drifting across a blue sky. Somewhere in the distance a mesmerizing tune was playing. Within moments, as if by magic, the clouds parted and two of my cats appeared. Katzenberg looked quite dapper in his tuxedo, and Witch-Hazel wore a can-can costume reminiscent of those French Riviera dancers. As I remember it, Katz was trying to teach Witch-Hazel a new dance.

Upon awakening, I quickly realized that all of this was more than a dream because the tune that belonged to the dream was actually coming from the radio in the living room. I quietly tiptoed out of the bedroom and peered into the living room. And there, although my vision was blurred from sleep, I clearly saw my cats dancing.

Imagination enables us to enter worlds that would otherwise be closed to our view. It is the core of creativity.

Previously published on Diane Bell's Web site *(http://diabellalovescats.com/trop.htm)* and condensed for this book.

10

Majestic Felines

Spirituality and Your Inner Self

All of us have a spiritual component as well as a physical, emotional, and psychological aspect. Call it mind, soul, spirit—whatever—that component is the very core of you, empowered by and embedded in your innermost self, the powerhouse that fuels your existence, the enabler of all you think, do, or say. Our animal friends, particularly cats, sometimes touch us at that extraordinarily profound level of consciousness and awaken in us the virtues we need most—compassion, courage, perseverance, truth, justice, fortitude, temperance, patience, etc.

Even in their darkest hours, cats are majestic. They possess nobility of being, a regal quality that draws us to love them and share our lives with them. Cats stand tall, as it were, tail up with a little hook, moving gracefully through the universe, harmoniously attuned to it even in hardship, courageous in whatever befalls them, responsive ultimately to the goodness and kindness of strangers. They speak their truth by being true to their innermost being, that catness that makes them what they are.

Sister Diane once said to me, "Life is for you all the way, baby." Unexpected words for a nun, perhaps, but absolutely true in their meaning. Let your spiritual being find nourishment in everything you read, say, hear, and do. Your soul is manifest by the way you live. Practice meditation, prayer, and contemplation. Chant as your cat does when it purrs. Watch the cat and embrace your innermost self.

The Miracle of Akira

by Lisa Sanders

One cold and rainy Friday, I found Akira. She appeared to be about four months old and weighed little more than a pound. She had been mauled, and there were cuts on one side of her rib cage and a lump the size of a silver dollar on the other. She hung her head, uttered not a sound, and shivered violently. I thought I'd just nurse her back to health and find her a home. I didn't like cats, never had, and I didn't want one.

By Saturday she was up exploring the bathroom, her temporary home. I took Monday off and brought Akira to the vet, who struggled to keep from crying upon seeing her. She ordered a FeLV and FIV test, and the vet *did* cry when she said Akira had FeLV and her red blood cell (PCV) values were at fifteen—she should have been dead. The options were euthanasia or treatment, but by this time, there was no option. "Treat her!" I said.

The next week, Akira was full of life, determined to survive. At our next visit, the vet cried for joy. Akira gained almost a pound the first week and her PCV was going up.

An abscess a few days later was a terrible setback, but Akira is nine months old now, weighs seven pounds, and is a happy, healthy, nonanemic cat. She still is symptomatic for FeLV, but you'd never know it looking at her. My furry angel opened the eyes of my heart!

Every act of compassion refines your inner spirit and moves you forward on the path of enlightenment.

The Story of Mr. Jinx

by Margaret Ambler

Sometimes I wish I had never given Mr. Jinx that name. I was asked to take in four eight-week-old kittens that came from a farm, but it is very difficult to get feral kittens at this age to come around. One of the kittens was very wild, and for the first month, I didn't know if he was male or female.

I began feeding them little treats of ham, my secret weapon. At first, feral kittens will spit and slash out at you, but once they get a good taste of the ham, they are hooked. In a while, the whole group was successfully re-homed, except for the one little gray boy. I was somewhat worried, but I refused to give up on him. Several more weeks went by before he started to come around very slowly. Maybe humans were not so bad!

By the time he was nine months old and living with my cat gang and me, Mr. Jinx had become a great friend. Some time later, poor Mr. Jinx fell ill. I have never seen a cat go down so fast. Within twenty-four hours, Mr. Jinx was gone. He was only a year old.

I buried him at the top of the garden and planted a rose above his tiny grave. It was worth all our effort to earn his trust and friendship. From that day forward, I never turned my back on any needy feline. True, we can't save them all, but the little we do helps at least a few.

The courage of your convictions will enable you to persevere in doing good regardless of the outcome.

Teacher, Philosopher, and Wise Old Sage

by Ed Kostro

When my wife works at her desk, Buddha Buddy lies next to her, freely imparting his vast cosmic knowledge, thus enabling her to complete her tasks quickly and efficiently.

Our other felines, Monty, Jessie, Tuffy, and Gabby, constantly seek Buddha Buddy's guidance. When they bicker, Buddy steps in and soon manages to bring peace back into the fold, reestablishing harmony and love to our home.

Amazingly, Buddha Buddy's compassion and willingness to guide is not restricted to humans and felines. These days, you will also find him instructing two rather hyper, mischievous canine orphans named Blanca and Turbo. When they misbehave, Buddy gently scolds them and firmly explains that barking, biting, belching, stealing cat food, hiding bones in the litter box, and running amok through the house are definitely not the paths to nirvana.

Buddha Buddy—teacher, philosopher, wise old sage, and good friend.

The true teacher accepts disciples as they appear, without prejudice or false expectations.

Teaching Miracles and Soul Mates

by Lisa Sanders

Akira and her huge baby brother, Indy, are best friends, which is why I couldn't figure out the reason that he was biting her all of a sudden, in the late night, on her back. He was neutered, so I knew it couldn't be sexual.

Each time it happened, Akira let out a howl but never fought back. I decided to ask an animal communicator.

Mara spoke to Akira and Indy together. She said that Akira calls "spirits and energy" to her to help heal her, but poor Indy doesn't know what they are. All he sees are little "glow bugs" flying over her, and he wants to get them away from her. Akira howls because she can't move while she is in a trance. The animal communicator convinced Indy to stop, and he hasn't bitten his friend since.

Akira says she is on this earth to teach me and everyone else a "lesson about miracles," to protect me, and that she will always be with me, even in death. Mara described Akira's spirit as a magical and mythical soul like a unicorn's. Everyone who has been around this little FeLV+ kitten has been thrown back in awe of her energy.

Akira is a soul mate to me by her own definition, her heart and mine together. Some people call them familiars, but either way, it is a special bond that we are only so lucky to ever find again in our past, present, or future lives.

Surrounded by mystery, never judge what you do not fully comprehend. Strive to be reverent in the face of the great unknowns and to be grateful for every experience that deepens your consciousness of the mystery.

Sapphire's Pile of Cats

by Paul Sutton

Cats are known to be territorial and usually hate others being taken into their family, but we had one that loved all newcomers, a delightful little Siamese called Sapphire (Saffi).

We had five cats at the time. It was a treat to see them all together, when they would end up in a heap on the armchair cuddling around Ms. Saffi. It happened that way because she was simply so good-natured that they all gravitated to her for affection and piled one atop the other in the process. I hope you can picture the scene of two Siamese cats, one tabby cat, one black-and-white cat, and a tortoiseshell all really cuddling up so close to each other that it looked like one big funny-colored cat!

One time we had a very small ginger kitten to look after for a week. Saffi immediately became its Mum and would curl up with it for hours, tenderly licking its fur. It was a great disappointment that we couldn't breed Saffi because of cysts on her ovaries, but if ever a cat was made to have a family, it was Saffi.

Nurturing is a maternal instinct and a special talent that is not exclusive to biological moms.

Mollycoddle

by Barbara H. Vinson

Molly was one determined little cat. She was a blue tabby with a pretty face and a crooked spine, the self-appointed leader of a colony of strays in the Bronx. Nothing and nobody ever got the better of Miss Mollycoddle. But underneath it all, she was really a little sweetheart; she was bossy only because she was trying so hard to make a go of it. Fortunately for her and her companions, though, a kindhearted lady came every single day to feed them.

One day, Molly suddenly found herself on her way to the veterinarian. The kind-hearted lady wanted Molly checked over to see why she had such a crooked spine. Other than a rather severe case of spinal scoliosis, Dr. Johnson pronounced Molly in excellent health and put her up for adoption. I happened in just about then, fell instantly in love with her, and adopted her on the spot—one of the best things I've ever done for *myself*, let alone the adoptee.

Molly's the matriarch of my cat family. She'll still clock anybody who gets out of hand, but then she'll mother them, too—and so caringly.

Molly seems to possess a natural spirituality. Whenever she hears me chanting at my Buddhist altar, she'll make a beeline for my lap to claim her piece of the spiritual pie. She always stays with me till I've finished and the last candle is blown out.

No wonder nothing ever gets the better of Miss Mollycoddle.

Our spiritual practice is the underpinning of our whole life.

Grace

by Diana "Sue" Snyder

My Bengals love to play in the water, especially if I am taking a bath. They jump up on the edge of the tub, walk all around it, dip their tails in, and splash water with their paws. If I put a floating toy in the tub, they will bat it around for hours. This cast-iron, porcelain-covered bathtub has an incredibly slippery and hard surface. Needless to say, the cats can't use their claws to negotiate their ventures. Several have jumped up and gone kerplunk!

The other day, my very pregnant queen, Sheeba, placed her paws on the outer side of the tub and peered up at me bathing. She appeared ready to jump onto the edge of the tub for a quick visit. I said, "OK, girl, be careful! You're kinda big now. If you overshoot your jump, you're gonna go for a swim."

Sheeba gazed up at me with a look of understanding. Then she extended her body, stretching her huge belly as far as it would go, and hooked her front paws around the inside edge of the tub. In one smooth motion, her strong back legs gave a gentle bounce. Seemingly without effort, she pulled herself up, glancing indignantly over her shoulder.

I was astonished. Even at her size, she was poetry in motion, the epitome of elegance and grace.

Pregnancy never detracts from but rather enhances natural dignity and grace.

....

Pete and the Poodle

by Dana Smith-Mansell

Pete was a beautiful black-and-white domestic shorthair. His body was lean and his hair shone like silk. He was very laid-back in his demeanor and would often just meander gracefully across the lawn—nary a care in the world. He often just sat and watched the world, unaffected by anything that came in his vision.

Next door there lived a yappy toy poodle. She would bark at the wind if she had a mind to, and she always barked at Pete. Pete would be strolling across the yard, and if "the poodle" was anywhere in the vicinity, she would begin her taunting by yapping right behind Pete's backside. But Pete would just continue strolling along, seemingly unaware of this nuisance. This would occur daily.

Every once in a while Pete would develop a gleam in his eye and would almost appear to smile. Onlookers would watch with great anticipation. As the poodle yapped behind him, Pete would suddenly turn and stare her right in the eye. The poodle, who was shocked every time, would jolt and jump back almost frozen with fear. She would, however, quickly compose herself and head home with great speed. Pete would then place himself in a sitting position and begin to clean his paws. No stress, just triumph and sheer attitude!

Be nonchalant when you encounter teasing or any other sort of derisive behavior.

The Aristocat

by Theresa Mancuso

If you have never lived with a British shorthair, you've missed one of life's most inspiring experiences. Primo is slate gray in color, bluish even, with a plush coat of soft silk, and huge round copper-colored eyes, a glamour cat if ever there was one. As master and commander of all that he perceives, Primo struts about with that sense of dignity and nobility that mark an awesome presence.

Despite an occasional outburst of rage defending his territory from his tiger brother, Marmaduke Rodgers, the alley cat with a questionable background, Primo maintains an aloofness that has to be predicated on the historical fact that the great cats of Rome eventually made their way to Great Britain and thence to the other nations of the world. Primo has citizenship of another time and place, it seems, and he remains a genuine aristocat. Looking at him as he sits atop my computer or stands on the back of an armchair to survey the terrain, I marvel at his perfection of form and face. He enters a room to welcome guests, carrying his great tail aloft with the feline hook of pride at the end of it. "I'm a Cat's cat," he seems to say. Never stooping to hold a grudge, Primo is lord of the realm, seldom bothering to enforce his position, but when necessary, it's a duel of honor, not of passion.

Look inward for true strength and confidence.

Firestorm in California

by Kari Winters

National headlines told the tragic story of "Firestorm 2003." The parts they left out of the story were all of the remarkable tales of the ways in which animals helped during this horrible time.

I volunteer with California Siamese Rescue (CASR), and we got e-mails from people saying things like, "I have my cat I rescued from CASR to thank for nudging me awake and not letting me go back to sleep. He made such a commotion that I finally turned on the TV and found that the fire was huge and less than a mile away from where we lived."

My own house was never in danger, but the smoke was very thick at times. I was taking a nap when my cat, Nicky, wacked me very hard on the head. Because of past experiences with Nicky, when he whaps, I listen. I jumped up in bed but didn't see or hear anything unusual. I decided to look around the house, and when I got to my office, my other cat, King Tut, was having a very bad asthma attack and was unable to breathe. I grabbed him and got him into the bathroom to use his emergency inhaler, and he was able to breathe again. My veterinarian and I have no doubt that he would have died if Nicky hadn't awakened me.

Whoever said that cats are aloof and uncaring obviously never had one!

If we could be as loyal and caring as our pets, we would indeed be the kind of people we were meant to be.

Contemplative Cat

by Theresa Mancuso

Many years ago, when I was a young Sister assigned to the Cathedral School in Syracuse, New York, among my Sister companions there was a young nun who added a Buddhist touch to her Roman Catholic spirituality. Back in those days, I had not yet had the opportunity to understand what a great alliance the Buddhist practice can have with Christianity. So I was taken aback when I knocked on the Sister's door one evening after dinner to deliver a set of papers we had been working on.

She was sitting before a candle near the window, obviously in meditation, and since the door was slightly ajar, she invited me in without changing her position. I never forgot the peace that dwelt on her face and features in the flickering light of that single candle.

From the first day that Marmaduke lived with me, he had a great fascination with candles. I frequently light a large candle in the center of my dining room table or before religious icons around the room. Marmaduke immediately takes his place and quietly sits before the candle, staring very steadily at the flame, never moving, seeming not even to breathe, so still is his whole body. Usually, Marmaduke skids about like a wild man, but when the candles are lit, before I take my place, he takes his and gently, without meaning to, my red tiger shows me another aspect of meditation.

Meditation is a valuable spiritual practice.

Demelza

by Barbara H. Vinson

Demelza. Believe me, they only made one. How many cats do you know who, when you plant a kiss on one side of their head, they turn it for one on the other side? I think she'd spend half the day doing that, if I let her.

Demelza was the only black-and-white baby of four kittens born in Flushing, Queens, in my friend Janet's backyard. One day, the mother cat put all four kittens in a window well, where she knew Janet would find them and take them in. You see, the mother cat was very ill and could no longer care for her babies. She did come back later on to satisfy herself that the kittens had been taken; after that, she was never seen again.

Demelza was my very first black-and-white cat, named for Demelza from Winston Graham's *Poldark*. She is now eleven and a half years old, and it's so hard to believe. It seems only yesterday that she was an active, mischievous little kitten who taught all subsequent kittens the art of self-defense and play skirmishing. Even at this age, she's still very kitten-like—and certainly as spirited as her namesake—all in all, a four-legged blessing.

By all accounts Demelza should be the matriarch of our household but could care less about rank; she'd rather do her own thing and leave the "matriarching" to Molly!

To be genuinely loving, you must forget about yourself. Take up your daily life with purpose and perseverance and do not seek the first place or highest rank.

....

Jeremy

by Barbara H. Vinson

Jeremy was a stray until Patty rescued him and put him up for adoption. When I dropped by to see Patty one afternoon, there he sat, a handsome black-and-white cat, getting his ears scratched by a customer. She didn't adopt him, but I made up my mind right then and there that I would, and his name would be Jeremy. I loved the fact that even with all the noise and confusion in the pet shop, Jeremy was in heaven just because someone was scratching his ears.

When I brought him home, I could tell that Jeremy was anxious to be accepted by my other cats, but he needn't have worried. They liked him right away because he was so well mannered, abiding by all the new-cat-on-the-block rules.

I had just adopted a new kitten, Zeppelin, and Jeremy immediately appointed himself Zeppie's legal guardian. He washed Zep from stem to stern every single day. Zeppie was so clean he squeaked! I think his little meows said, *Enough already!* But Zeppie got his daily bath whether he wanted it or not.

Jeremy's been a member of the family for six years, an extremely lovable character who's gotten to be a bit of a feline Mack truck, weighing in at more than twenty-one pounds—and oh yes, absolutely—he's a lap cat.

Love is a light that shines in the darkness, a beacon for life's journey. Be that light.

11

The Eternal Wisdom of Cats

Seeking the Meaning of Life

Anthropologists tell us that many so-called "primitive" societies deeply respect the wisdom of their elders. In our materialistic society, so often tragically lacking in spiritual depth, not only are the elderly treated with disregard, but wisdom itself is often unappreciated.

Wisdom comes slowly, drop by drop in the flow of experience; suffering brings the largest drops of insight and wisdom. A life without meaning is useless. Wisdom understands the significance and meaning of many seemingly insignificant meaningless words, actions, and events. Wisdom opens the mind to grasp essence rather than appearance.

Wisdom sees beyond sophistication and prejudice to the real heart of things. Wisdom observes and listens and takes time to assimilate the truth. Wisdom does not jump to conclusions. Wisdom restrains mouth and voice against impulsive words and rash statements. Wisdom avoids actions that will be regretted later. It creates gentleness and firmness. It molds our ability to consider from many perspectives, to listen and reflect, and to wait for the right moment.

Wisdom grapples with eternal questions without running away in frustration or despair. Wisdom realizes that understanding comes slowly and teaches us patience and perseverance. Wisdom says: "Give your life everything you've got, but when it's time to give your soul back to God, do it willingly, with gratitude. 'Thank you, I had a wonderful time! Glad I could be here.'"

Are Cats or Dogs the Cat's Meow?

by Paulette Cooper

I once had a furry gray and white Persian and a furry gray and white Shih Tzu at the same time; both were the same size. Unless I looked at their faces close enough to count the whiskers or note if they had any, I couldn't tell whether I was looking at my dog or my cat.

To complicate matters, my cat played fetch, bringing balls back to my feet; she slept at the foot of my bed, drank out of the toilet bowl, and talked to me, especially to tell me when she wanted to eat. When my dog became old, in her doggie dotage, she mainly slept, ignoring me when she was awake—exactly what people say cats do!

I decided to do some research on dog and cat attributes to compare the two. Cats, it turns out, make ten times more vocal sounds than dogs, watch moving objects better, run faster, have better peripheral vision, are more dexterous with their paws, and have more sophisticated taste buds.

Dogs have more sophisticated olfactory senses and can therefore smell (and track) better, are superior herders, and can usually understand their humans better. Most dual pet owners, like me, feel that their dogs and cats are equally wonderful, and it's been said (tactfully) that you can't compare the two anyway because dogs are better at being dogs, and cats are better at being cats. Except for my two, who were a bit confused.

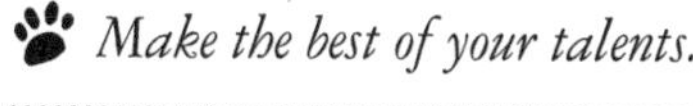

Make the best of your talents.

Beyond Fear and Doubt

by Lauren L. Merryfield

There were cats in my family for many years. Cats who know me always figure out that I cannot physically see. Although they may test me as kittens, they always get beyond the doubt and questioning. For them, I become the person they trust most.

Whether I can see as they do or not is forgotten; it is placed where it belongs in the hierarchy of things to worry about, near the bottom. Humans, most of the time, show some amount of fear or doubt just looking at me. I can almost hear their brains churning (or maybe it's their stomachs!).

"You can't do . . ." or "How do you . . . ?" or "Who does . . . for you?" "You have to be able to see to do that . . ." "You'd be a risk as a volunteer because of . . ."

Nearly every cat I've ever lived with has learned to be helpful when I drop something. Their egos never seem to get involved. They do not seem to feel superior to me (as some humans do) because they can see. Nor do they show pity like people do. They just simply come to me for everything they need.

Never treat people differently because of physical challenges.

Setting the Record Straight

by Jackie S. Brooks

All our cats were fantastic mothers, but Trixie was exceptional. She could not have kittens, but she desperately wanted babies of her own—so much so that she kit-napped two of our other cats' kittens from a basket in our living room.

I found out after I saw Trixie acting rather furtively, slinking away and crawling under a garden shed. I checked on the kittens and realized two had gone missing while their mother was out answering the call of nature. The kittens were only a few days old. I went to the shed and listened and heard their squeaks as she "talked" to them. We had to rip up floorboards to reach them, and then I returned them to their mother.

Trixie was frantic; she wailed and howled, so eventually I put her, the mother, and the kittens upstairs. I made sure she could not get out of the house with them again, but from that moment on, she was content. Trixie developed milk for them, and she and the mother took it in turns to nurse the kittens.

They were the first of Trixie's adored adopted babies. She gave unconditional love to many more.

There are so many marvels in nature that when we stop to consider even the smallest of them, it often staggers the mind, always uplifts the spirit, and never ceases to amaze us.

Primo, the First of All Cats

by Theresa Mancuso

No matter what goes on in our family, Primo is totally aware, but he remains aloof and seldom gets involved. Is it that he's timid? I used to wonder. Is he detached? As a kitten, Primo was fearless. He was inquisitive with visiting canines of every size, venturing so close that he came nose-to-nose with them, and loved to strut his stuff before admiring human guests. But when Marmaduke Rodgers and Charlie came to live with us, Primo took a new posture in our home. Like the Buddha, Primo contemplates and considers. No longer a kitten, he is free of the impulse to race forward and inquire who is arriving when the door opens to welcome visitors. He watches and waits, the first of all cats, but not in need of your attention, thank you very much.

Later, in his own good time, the contemplative cat approaches, butting a luxuriously furry head and shoulder against your ankle or wrist. *Hey, there, I'm Primo.* When I am at the computer, Primo wraps his arms around my left wrist, lays his head on my hand, and purrs majestically. He rolls over on his back and stretches out with all four paws in the air, at home in the midst of dogs, cats, and other species, people included. His place in the universe totally secure, Primo looks out at the world with wise copper-colored eyes from a beautiful round face covered with a thick plush coat of slate blue gray. Il Primo di Tutti Gatti, Finalmente Arrivato.

When you find your home in the universe, accepting your place in the scheme of things, content with who you are and what you must do, true happiness flows. Consider this, and be at peace wherever you are.

Chagall After Dark

by Louise Maguire

When it gets dark, Chagall sits by the door. Coaxing, pleading, imploring, he cries.

I've business I must be about. There are interlopers to rout. Please let me out, me out, me out.

I argue with him.

"My cosseted cat, is it wise for you to duel with the outside feline world, to challenge rivals to bitter fights, to exchange these savage screams and more than vicious scratches and bites?"

Already in spirit, he is one with owl and bat in a world beyond human understanding. His wide eyes search my face, knowing.

"My pitch-black cat, must I release you to be one with the inky night? Can your jade eyes challenge the star-bright heavens?"

His sleek shape has subtly altered, toughened, every hair electrified. His tail rises and bristles. I sense his feral voice reply, deeper, hoarser, closer to the wild tiger within him. Without words, his looks and gestures speak to me: *I adore you, my mistress. By day I will comfort and accompany you, pampered and petted as your beloved friend. But my love of the night is a deeper passion. It is the ultimate nature of Cat.*

And so I open the door to satisfy his primitive desires and Chagall moves into the darkness.

"May you return safely once more, dew-pearled in the morning light."

"Know thyself," said Socrates. Be true to your nature, your innermost self. Do not be deterred by that which is less perfect. Listen to your heart.

....

Reach Out and Touch Someone

by Theresa Mancuso

Having recently acquired a new Apple PowerBook, and having been duly warned by experienced friends of the dangers to the delicate keyboard, and knowing the propensity of my cat-kids to leap wherever my eyes focus or my hands touch, I determined to work in the silence of my bedroom, with door closed and cats on the other side! Ah, safety for the Mac and silence for my concentration!

Alas, the vocal demonstration about this unacceptable prohibition began immediately with yelps, howls, and melodious meows. The volume mounted, but I would not yield. The cats serenaded me with their protest chorus for at least half an hour. I, such a pushover for animals, felt duly proud that I had not succumbed to their insistence.

My work continued. I stayed the course. The screeching continued, too, until suddenly, there came an abrupt end to the feline demo and everything grew silent and still. Had they all died of heart attacks or stroke from verbal excess? Looking up from the monitor, my eyes swept the room. Perhaps they had slid under the door like steamrollered cats and were in fact *inside*? Yikes!

But no, not so. Instead, six furry hands were reaching under the door at the same time: a gray pair belonging to Primo, a deep orange pair belonging to Marmaduke Rodgers, and tiny Charlie's snow white paws.

Never allow yourself to be too busy to reach out and touch someone.

Finding a Voice

by Theresa Mancuso

Animal sounds have always intrigued me, from my earliest memories of listening to the birds that lingered in my mother's lilac bushes outside my bedroom window, to my present-day hobby of mimicking the language of my own cats and dogs. Indeed, I believe I may have nearly perfected my cat voice, along with my doggie growl and yelp.

My cat voice consists of a large repertoire of sounds that I have copied from my feline roommates over the last twenty years or more. At first, this seemed the natural thing to do, as a human will coo and gurgle over an infant. I mewed and purred over my cat kids, copying their tonal qualities and hoping that I was not saying anything forbidden by feline etiquette. Truth be told, I actually enjoy the sound of animal voices that have become part of my own vocabulary, and my pets respond by rhythmically twitching their tails or bobbing their foreheads against my own. They know the lingo well, and they seem to appreciate that I've taken the time and trouble to learn their native tongue.

Recently, I visited friends who are also cat people. They share their home with two adopted feline princesses rescued years ago and ardently beloved. The purpose of my visit was to photograph their cats for a calendar. In their beautiful guest bedroom, I paused on all fours, crouching on the plush carpeted floor trying to capture an eye-level portrait of Misty, a gorgeous gray feline equal in beauty to my sophisticated British shorthair. I meowed splendidly with all the passion of a Pavarotti aria and purred softly with the tenderness of Leontyne Price's rendering of Gounod's "Ave Maria."

While Misty was not greatly moved by my vocalization, her companion Brandy was. Perched atop a mirror-fronted wardrobe, the large red tabby stalked her way forward and hung her head over the front, paying me the utmost attention. *Another meow ought to do it,* I thought, and sure enough, *con boca aperta* (with an open mouth), I captured Brandy's beautiful face reflected in the mirror, her eyes shining. She had found a friend, and I had found my feline voice!

Practice your "thing" until it becomes your "bliss."

What Goes Around . . .

by Lillian Howell

My great-grandma Mary always loved cats, but her sister Lizzie was never fond of them. Mary called her cat Musty, but Lizzie came up with a few other names for it. Musty, a beautiful tabby, lived in the kitchen and had great talent as a mouser. One day Lizzie called on her sister on her way from town. They settled down for a cup of tea and a chat, as sisters do.

Now, cats are curious. If you open a cupboard, they crawl right in. If you leave a suitcase open, they'll sit inside of it on top of all your clean clothes. (I nearly lost a kitten once because it crept into the empty space behind the storage drawer under the bed. I closed the drawer and heard the bed meowing.)

As any self-respecting member of the feline community would do, Musty decided to investigate Lizzie's shopping bag. He sniffed at it, and Lizzie kicked him away with some choice words. Musty was not used to this sort of treatment. Mary remonstrated with her, but Lizzie was unapologetic.

After finishing their tea, Lizzie stood up to go. She leaned down and found the inside of her shopping bag soaking wet—Musty's response to Lizzie's kick. It didn't do much for the food in the bag. Mary had fits of laughter and repeated the story for weeks afterwards at Lizzie's expense. Poor Lizzie never did see the funny side.

What goes around, comes around.

Akira's Canine Pal

by Lisa Sanders

Introducing Akira to my dogs Lancelot and Bow Tie had been hit and miss. At first, I thought all would go well since Akira curled up next to my Dachshund (Lance) and went to sleep. Next time, however, she became a wild lady, spitting, swatting, and running away. It's been like that ever since.

I kept the dogs crated when they were in her room, so eventually Akira came out from under the bed to explore. She relaxed and accepted them, so I let them out of their crates on leashes. Back went Akira under the bed.

She finally tolerated the dogs on leash, but still hissed, batted their noses, and ran for protection. Still, we were getting somewhere. The big test was turning them loose. Akira didn't like it. Back on their leashes if one of them came anywhere near her, Akira would run and hide. Bow Tie could care less, but Lance wanted to be friends.

One day, I was sitting on the floor with Lance in my lap. In came Akira: *Sniff, sniff.* Lance's tail wagged a mile a minute. He sniffed her back. Up went her tail straight into the air. She stayed put as Lance went toward her, then raced off. He made chase. Suddenly—an amazing turnabout! Lancelot tore past me in *front* of the cat! Tail at full mast, Akira pounced on him, then turned and scooted the other way with dog in tow. Never did I see such a sight! Now, forevermore, they're best friends.

Little by little, day by day, we're getting better and better. Perseverance is the key to achievement.

An Indelible Mark

by Paul Sutton

I am "animal mad"—our family always had cats. When I was about sixteen, we got a special cat named Sally that was ready to have kittens, and I was very excited. I had never seen anything being born before. When her water broke, we all gathered round and watched her little body as it strained to give birth. After a while, my Mum realized that Sally was in trouble.

We rushed her to the vet, where she had to have an emergency caesarean due to a blockage. The vet found that a dead kitten was prohibiting the passage of the rest of the litter. Somehow the vet managed to breathe life into this little soul and deliver the two others safely. My Mum, my sister, and I hand-reared one kitten each—not easy, but they all survived and flourished. Needless to say, none of us could part with our own special baby, so we kept them all. We had four other cats at the time, but since we lived on a farm, there was plenty of room around the garden and farmyard for them. I'm proud to say they all lived into a great old age, but I will never forget feeding them from tiny droppers for the first few weeks of their lives. I felt a very special bond with Amber, my pale ginger kitten, big, fluffy, and very cuddly. Any animal that you have loved, and that has loved you, leaves an indelible mark on your life. I feel privileged to have owned them all.

When we nurture others, we nurture ourselves as well.

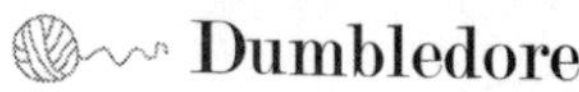

Dumbledore

by Barbara H. Vinson

Dumbledore, believe it or not, was a throwaway. That's right. I heard that some neighbors down the road abandoned him after bringing home a new kitten, and it was their neighbor who dropped by to ask me if I'd take Dumbledore. She explained that she feeds feral cats and Dumbledore had been declawed. She was afraid that the ferals would make mincemeat out of him if a skirmish ensued. I said I would gladly take him—sight unseen. I am a sucker for a cat, especially a cat in need.

Dumbledore is the quintessential "noble beastie"—a handsome blue tabby with aqua eyes as big as nickels and the gentlest, sweetest of personalities. He has a long head, a long nose, a long body, long legs, and a long tail. When he came to us, he was very angular and somewhat underweight—like one of Steinlen's cat sketches—but now he's all filled out and has a beautiful, thick, glossy coat from vigorous good health. He's the "free spirit" of our household, for he loves the outdoors, but he also appreciates the warmth and comfort of his home on a cold winter's night.

He's very well named—every inch the wizard, the caster of magic spells! Believe me, I *know,* for I find myself happily acquiescing to his every whim, and he doesn't even have to bother with a wand!

🐾 *A life of kindness and compassion is what truly fills our emptiness and makes us complete and whole.*

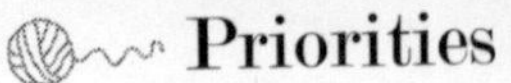

Priorities

by Catherine Miller

After our adventure outdoors, Curly dragged me up to his favorite haunt on the third floor. I had never seen a cat run up flights of stairs as fast as he did, pulling me with all the might of a sled dog. He collapsed, panting on the floor from exhaustion, relief, or a little of both. How much greater was his charismatic energy and vitality now than it had been then!

You might think his recent negative experience venturing into the world outside his den would have humbled him, but by sundown of that unforgettable day, when I next encountered Curly, it was as though he had conveniently forgotten the entire experience. There he was, sauntering about as confidently as ever, ready to welcome me and drag me aloft. He rearranged my body to suit him, looking down at the world outside from his vantage point at the window, king of the beasts once again.

For Curly, my king, the world is a wonderful place, even if he shied away a bit from meeting it head on. Give him his kingdom, give him his queen, and he is master and commander.

It's a mark of wisdom to balance one's life by establishing priorities that take into consideration one's own strengths and weaknesses, as well as those of others.

My First Cat

by Paul Sutton

One of my earliest memories of pets in our family was our cat, Tinker. He was black and very, very fluffy. He was more like a dog than a cat and always extremely affectionate. My two sisters and I went to a primary school that was only about a quarter of a mile up the hill from our house on the farm. It was a real village school, very small, and had only two teachers, one of whom was the headmistress. It was obvious that our headmistress was a cat lover because Tinker used to follow us to school every day, without fail, and he was always permitted to sleep in the staff room all through the morning. Tinker would follow us home for lunch, then back again for the afternoon session.

At the end of the term, our beloved cat was given special mention for having the best attendance record at school. The headmistress even sent Christmas cards addressed to Tinker and Shandy (our dog). I can see Tinker now, just a little way behind us toddling along, and if we called him, his tail would shoot up like a bottle brush and he'd run to catch up with us. How we loved our cat. None of the other kids had an animal that followed them to school. We felt very special, and so we were!

Memories of love are precious.

The Baptism

by Patti Thompson

Religious rituals are sometimes a puzzlement to adults. Try to explain to a six-year-old the reason why one would go into a church, climb into a room with a large basin filled with water, and let someone dunk you. I thought I had brought this experience down to her level, but apparently I left something out.

Cayla decided that our new kitten, Mary Phyllis, with her black and white fur, looked like a nun, so she renamed her Sister Verry Merry Phyllis. The two quickly bonded, and Cayla loved to take her nightly bath with Sister Phyllis perched on the edge of the tub.

One night we returned home from watching a baptism. Sister Phyllis and Cayla retired to the bathroom and began their nightly bath ritual. I tiptoed to the door to check on her and heard, "In the name of my father and a holy ghost, I baptize you Sister Phyllis," and with that, the splashing and hissing began! Cayla was trying to baptize Sister Phyllis! The soaked cat dashed past me and headed for parts unknown to escape from the bewildered and slightly scratched kid she left behind in a tub of bubbles.

Sister Phyllis didn't seem to suffer from her brush with religion, but we noticed that her ritual did. She no longer sat on the edge of the tub with Cayla. She sat entrenched in and protected by the bathroom sink across the room.

Ritual helps us get beyond our ordinary mind and enter a sacred space.

Just Good Friends

by Lyn McConchie

It was mid-March, and I was wandering through the house one evening around dusk. The fire was burning brightly, cooking up the piglet's barley. The door into the big enclosed cat park attached to the house was open to let some of the heat out, and Tiger was in the park schmoozing with Dancer—or so I thought until I wandered back the other way. Yes, that was Tiger, but who was this critter sitting on the back of the settee? Dancer!

Hang on a minute, if that was Dancer inside, then who was it sitting out in the cat park with Tiger? I drifted into the bedroom, collected a torch, strolled back to the cat park door, and shone the torch, moving the beam slowly so it wouldn't spook the stranger. The whatever-it-was eyed me doubtfully. Tiger-sized, furry, not too bothered so long as I approached no further, and . . . yes, we had a young brush-tailed opossum.

I sat on the step and spoke gently, and Tiger rushed up to be cuddled while the opossum hung back anxiously. I would have given him food, but the last thing I needed was the house invaded by opossums looking for handouts. When I looked later, he or she had gone again. Out of the park and off.

Tiger looked disconsolate. He had liked his new friend. He seemed to ask, "Are you sure you don't want a house-opossum?" I am and so, I suspect, is the opossum, but Tiger isn't so certain.

Trying out new experiences is a good way to stay young—that is, if you know your limits!

Miss Mitey Mitts

by Barbara H. Vinson

Scenario: a veterinarian's office in Flushing, Queens, on a busy Saturday afternoon. Clients wait patiently with their pets.

Enter: a little boy carrying a box. He places the box carefully on the floor. Suddenly, he flies out of the door and vanishes!

The box sits there. Then a staff member decides she'd better check it out. She does so, and inside sits a two-week-old polydactyl kitten.

All hearts went out to the little mite. She was carefully nursed, and she slept and ate a lot, the way all baby creatures do. But as she got older, she demanded more attention than anyone really had time to give her. It was time to find her a home.

Thank heavens "home" was to be with me. And how did the kitten come by the name of Mitey Mitts? Well, the night my friend Vivian came over to meet her and coo over her, the little dickens got it in her head that Vivian was going to medicate her. There was no way she was going to suffer *that* without protest, so she clocked Vivian soundly across the nose with one of her big white mitts!

Today, Mitts is grown—a handsome, golden-eyed black-and-white cat. She is also one of the most intelligent, caring creatures I have ever known. Bless the little boy who brought her in that day. Not only did he save her life, he gave a gift that kept on giving.

When we give generously to others, without realizing it, we are giving to ourselves, for generosity is its own reward.

Poppa Knows Best

by Fran Pennock Shaw

Poppa Cat was the biggest orange tabby I'd ever seen. A feral adult living in the field behind my house, he was obviously a successful hunter. He must have weighed fifteen pounds.

Poppa usually came with two small juveniles to share the feast I put out daily to trap them. I finally caught, neutered, and released them, never expecting Poppa to hang around. Maybe the kids would, I thought, but Poppa is much too smart to ever return to the site of his capture.

Silly me. It was the youngsters who eventually wandered off to claim their own territory, while Poppa steadfastly showed up for his free meal day after day, week after week, stretching into the next season. He took up residence under my deck, waited at my back steps for me to appear with food, and began snoozing, meowing, and rolling on his back in my presence.

One day, Poppa came purposely to where I sat reading, rubbed his chubby body against my leg, and let me stroke his immaculate fur. He sat down at my back door and waited. Clearly, he wanted in. He'd made up his mind. It was time for a change.

You pick your friends, they say, but you're stuck with your family. Poppa Cat showed me a different way to gracefully grow with life. He chose his family and made them his friends.

Friends are the family we make for ourselves.

Cat in a Tree

by Rod Marsden

There was a cat in a tree. It was a domestic ginger that might be found in any suburb of Sydney. What made this cat and this tree unusual was the locale. You see, they were in the middle of the "bush"—the outback of Australia.

It was a nature special. This great, lumbering Aussie with a great, lumbering attitude toward teasing deadly snakes was after the most destructive of beasties—the feral cat.

They were looking in southern Queensland and northern New South Wales, and they weren't having much luck; the ferals were too good at concealment. Eventually, the great, lumbering Aussie star and his crew decided to go in for some creative flimflammery. If they couldn't get a large, superbly muscled wild feline, they'd settle for a tamer, thinner domestic.

Hence, we have this domestic ginger up a tree being taken down by our star/hero. He's wearing gloves so as not to get scratched to death. The cat's looking bored. Just how many times was she put up the tree and taken down before the director yelled, "Cut! It's a wrap"? Only the cat and our star could say for sure, and they're not talking. By the way, a wild one that knows how to hide and is faster than the average human is generally too smart to scoot up a tree when there are so many better avenues of escape from its pursuers.

For some things, there is just no substitute.

Look Before You Leap

by Miriam Stewart

Our precious cat of twelve years has many special places she likes to sit and look out the window of our home. One of those spots I am sure she claims as her own is the top of our laundry hamper in our bedroom. This gives her a view of the backyard, with the flower garden and the many birds that visit there.

One summer evening after I had gotten into bed, the cat made her usual visit to her special spot. She jumped on the chair and then up onto the hamper. One small problem: The lid had been left up when it was used last. The cat disappeared into the hamper. The surprised cat finally stuck her head up and very gingerly jumped out of the empty hamper. I laughed so hard my side hurt.

I reflected back on my own life and wondered about the times I might have jumped right into the middle of something, and maybe I looked as foolish as my cat because I had not taken time to look before I jumped.

Never leap without looking; know the season and the time that is right for every purpose.

12

Time to Say Goodbye

Letting Go

No matter how long they live, the final parting with loved ones—be they human or animal—is always difficult. Coming to terms with life's ephemeral nature is not an easy task. Grief, with cruel rigor, can be just as compelling for a pet as for a person, and everyone who has loved and lost a beloved animal friend knows this fact all too well. Everything that lives must die.

When it's time to say goodbye, our feline friends are teachers to the end. They take in stride nature's way and seem to understand that mortality stalks every creature on the earth. Death's finality is difficult and universal. Letting go is the only certain way of surviving the loss of those we love, not that we surrender them easily. Letting go means accepting reality for what it is. The stark truth of our own short existence requires that we, too, must finally separate from everything and everyone we love. The strength to die well is only possible if we have learned to live well. Such is the truth of this world. From my cats, I have learned much about death, dying, and letting go.

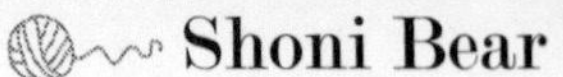

Shoni Bear

by Angela London

Shoni Bear was the best cat in the whole world. He was a fluffy blond and very laid back. He never complained about a thing. Bear and I lived in Wasilla, Alaska, for a short year and a half, his entire life. His first winter there averaged twenty degrees below zero outside and I had only wood heat in my home. One evening, I went to see a movie forty minutes away from where I lived. Bear was just a kitten then, maybe eight weeks old. I didn't want him to get cold, so I put him in my down parka and brought him with me. He was such an easygoing kitten, I knew I could get away with taking him. About ten minutes into the movie, I could hear this loud simultaneous purring and crunching when I accidentally dropped popcorn down the front of my parka. By the end of the movie, Bear was fast asleep.

A little over a year later, Bear was attacked by a neighbor dog on my property. He never complained, even when I felt him for injuries. The only way I knew he was injured was that he had a slight limp several days after the attack. After undergoing exploratory surgery, the vet said he had an infection. He was injured internally and had a broken leg. It was too late to save him. Bear was my best cat, and I still miss him.

It is truly better to have loved and lost than not to have loved at all.

Nikki's Final Resting Place

by Theresa Mancuso

Who would have ever expected the fragile Tonkinese kitten whose mother had died so young of respiratory disease to live out her eighteen-plus years with such vitality and vigor? Nikki was a super cat throughout her lifetime. From the age of twelve weeks, when I brought her home, there was not a single night that I did not wear her wrapped around my head throughout the night like a beloved earmuff.

Only on the last night of her life did Nikki wander forth to die by herself not far from my side. In the morning, I felt the heavy hammer of grief, but I could not complain, for Nikki's life was rich in love and happiness. She was much adored by her furry family, and her best friend, the Siamese Maximus, had already preceded her into the net of eternity. I wrapped the tiny corpse in an old T-shirt and drove out to the edge of town, where I buried her in a field beside a tree. It was a place I visited regularly to exercise my dog. Notwithstanding weather conditions or the passage of time, whenever we return to that site, my German shepherd, whose faithful companion Nikki had been throughout her lifetime, goes directly to the unmarked grave beside that small tree and stands reverently until I, too, reach the spot, and we lovingly remember a cat who was the best friend anyone could ever desire.

Visits to the graves of those who have passed away provide relief from the long night of separation.

Time to Say Goodbye

by Brenda Colbourne

After Cassanova's seventh surgery, I could not relax and believe that the surgery had finally been successful, so we just lived from day to day, trying to limit all expectations. Re-homing him had always been at the back of my mind, but I was scared to place him anywhere after so many setbacks. A friend of mine said that she was asking around for a suitable home, but I wasn't worried, as I did not think it would be difficult to re-home such a completely wonderful cat.

Then one day, I got a phone call from a lady looking for a male kitten. As I had two little ones, she decided to come over with her daughter to see them. Cassanova put on such a performance, it was embarrassing! He obviously knew something I didn't know because they left with Cassanova and not with a kitten as planned.

Recently, I've been able to visit Cassanova in his wonderful new home where he is very much loved and has everyone twisted around his paw. The luscious blue color has returned to his fur and it's so silky that it's amazing! I left him feeling great happiness and thinking that it was worth every cent of the money it had cost to have such an incredibly happy outcome.

When you go through a lot with someone, it's hard to say goodbye and move on, but nothing is forever, and letting go must happen over and over again before we reach our final destination.

Sheena

by Karen Heist

My first three cats died too soon, but when I got my fourth kitten just before going to college, Mom took care of it while I was away and the darling seemed to thrive. I named her Sheena. In my last year at school, I got a second cat called Sudia.

When I brought Sudia home from college, Sheena took off for an entire day. When she returned, she let everyone know how mad she was.

One Friday night, I nearly burned down the kitchen by overheating oil. Then Sheena knocked over a bottle of laundry detergent into my brother's clothes. We saw large bubbles coming out the window, landing in the neighbor's yard, the result of Sheena's adventure with the laundry soap. Home was a scene from *The Brady Bunch*.

Eventually, Sheena sweetened up, but last January she died, just short of her nineteenth birthday. I'm glad I'd spent many hours the day before holding and stroking her. How sad and empty it feels to lose a friend.

Memories keep loved ones alive in our heart long after they are gone.

Maximus and Cara Mia

by Theresa Mancuso

My oldest German shepherd, Cara Mia, was a large black female, almost a perfect bicolor. She was oversized at ninety pounds of muscle and large bone. I already had Maximus when Cara Mia joined our family, and as a small pup, she readily fell in love with Max, who loved her back. They cuddled together, played tag, and chased tennis balls all around my apartment. Max swatted every behavioral mishap the puppy ever got into, and as an adult dog, Cara Mia greatly respected her kitty pack buddy. Eventually, another cat and another dog joined the pack, but when Cara Mia's hindquarters deteriorated due to hip dysplasia, it became necessary to relieve her of her misery by gently putting her to sleep. Accompanied by my friend Mary, both of us with heavy hearts, we took my big girl to the vet and returned home that night with a small oak urn that contained her ashes.

Maximus met us at the door and followed us to the dining room table, where I placed the box of ashes. Immediately, the Siamese leaped to the top of the table and circled the urn several times, sniffing carefully and considering. Round and round Maxi went, never taking her eyes or nose off the urn. Then, in a surprise maneuver, the tiny cat climbed up on the urn and lay there with her legs wrapped around it and her belly flat on its top surface as if she were trying to embrace her old friend.

We can face the pain of loss better if we are willing to express our sorrow honestly in whatever manner suits our character and the circumstances in which we find ourselves.

Saving Tammy

by Theresa Mancuso, with help from Lois Goldstene

My friend Lois faithfully feeds strays and ferals in several Brooklyn locations. The day we met, Lois told me that she was particularly concerned about a cat she and Miriam, another neighborhood angel, had tried to catch for many months. They had caught its littermates, neutered or spayed them, and released them (a humane method for feline population control). They had been feeding Precious and Tammy since the cats were about four months old—nearly three years! Eager to vet and re-home these furry knights of the road, Lois was downhearted about Tammy, who was now exceedingly pregnant.

With all the qualities of a beloved housecat, Tammy never had a chance until one spring night, just before suppertime, Lois's friend Miriam successfully caught the mother-to-be, scooped her up, and took her to their friend Judy's house, where a nursery was prepared for her delivery. The next day Tammy gave birth to six healthy kittens. The loving care they are receiving at Judy's has helped Tammy and her family thrive. Tammy the feral cat is now Tammy the tame. The search for a permanent home is underway while Tammy continues to nurse her little ones and train them to use their litter box, which is so essential in preparing for a home of their own. A good mother, Tammy is a lucky cat. Her guardian angels never gave up; Tammy and her babies will never be feral again.

Chinese wisdom says: "It is better to light one candle than to curse the darkness." Many lament the legions of feral cats, but too few do something about it.

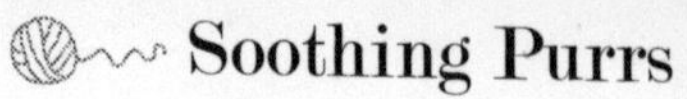

Soothing Purrs

by Toni and Ed Eames

Although Cameo and my beloved guide dog Ivy lived together for six years, they could not be called friends. When the day came for me to make that dreaded call to ask our veterinarian to euthanize thirteen-year-old Ivy, Cameo sprang into action. This fourteen-year-old tuxedo cat flung herself into my arms with a clear message that she felt my pain and was there to comfort me. With tears rolling down my face, I sat on the floor stroking Ivy.

Cameo shared her ministrations with her long-term house partner by walking back and forth between the two of us, purring loudly and stopping periodically to lick Ivy's face, something she never did before.

When the vet arrived, we sat on the floor in a circle around Ivy to provide comfort in her last moments. At this time, Cameo was fast asleep in her favorite chair. Waking with a start and sensing our need, the sound of Cameo's tinkling bell alerted me that help was on the way. Cameo jumped over my husband Ed and joined the circle to provide the comfort we so desperately sought in this emotion-laden crisis. As I held Ivy in my arms and reached down to touch her, I felt Cameo's tiny paw touching Ivy's large paw. Cameo seemed incredibly attuned to the importance of this touch since Ivy was now totally blind. The last sounds my treasured teammate heard were my sobs and Cameo's soothing purrs as Ivy slipped quietly into a sweet and painless death.

At the time of death, the person who is passing on as well as close friends and family will be comforted and strengthened by the communal presence.

Marmaduke Rodgers Is Saying His Prayers

by Theresa Mancuso

When I met Marmaduke Rodgers, I was in my "white cat era," completely fascinated by the beauty of white felines. I don't know why I was so drawn to him. I was nowhere near thinking I'd adopt another pet. But as life would have it, the "tiny tiger" chortled away as he climbed the sides of his cage and moved right into my heart. There are things we do from reason and things we do from impulse, but the greatest things of all are those we do from love. Taking Marmaduke Rodgers home was a simple act of love.

He needed me; he needed a *forever* home. He had been bounced around quite enough, thank you. And on some deep spiritual level, I needed him, too. Into our lives came the furry gangster-saint, Marmaduke Rodgers, destined to win everybody's heart. Once you meet our friendly red giant, you quickly fall in love with him, gangster-saint that he is, a cat making mischief just by waking up and, just as ably, soothing the hurts and sorrows of life by quietly settling down! Marmaduke's sweet chirps sound like the whispered prayers of old ladies mumbling their Hail Marys as they pray their rosaries in the back of the church. They love the sight of candle flames and so does Marmaduke Rodgers.

One day I realized that Marmaduke had his own way of saying his prayers, as he perched before an icon, chortling away, or stood silent on the windowsill, watching doves fly by (white pigeons, actually). *Chortle. Chortle. Bless the beasts and children.* Prayer doesn't change God; it changes us. And sure enough, when tiny kitten

Charles was rescued, it was gangster-saint Marmaduke that took over his care and early training. Master Monk in Red.

Prayer is the lifting of our hearts and minds to worship, praise, and adore.

....

Mr. Nasty's Obituary

by Mercedes M. Cardona

FOREST HILLS, QUEENS—Mr. Nasty Cardona died at the Forest Hills Cat Hospital in Glendale, Queens, after a two-month battle with cancer. He was twelve. The cause of death was euthanasia, said Dr. Jay Luger, who had treated the pugnacious Persian since he was found wandering the streets of Manhattan in the summer of 1992.

"He was the most beautiful cat I'd ever seen. He was also the meanest cat I've ever seen," said his rescuer, Susan Avery. Unable to control him, she arranged to transport him to a shelter, until he was befriended by fellow cat Ms. Kitty Cardona and moved to a new adoptive home in Queens.

During the following decade, Mr. Nasty became well known at the Forest Hills Cat Hospital for his high-strung temperament. Several attempts were made to control his rage, including an experiment with Valium, which failed when he demonstrated his ability to hang by his teeth from his human's hand. In spite of his quirks, the ferocious feline was beloved by many, who looked past the hissing and growling and enjoyed his feats of shadowboxing and his ability to chase his own tail—and often catch it.

Since being diagnosed with cancer, Mr. Nasty tried to keep up his former activities, but the rapidly growing tumor in his mouth made biting difficult. He managed a brief spot of growling and hissing before his final appointment with Dr. Luger. Mr. Nasty is survived by Ms. Kitty and by their human, Mercedes Cardona, both of Forest Hills.

Everything that lives must die. Make peace with mortality, especially your own.

Life After William

by Louise Maguire

Again John hadn't tasted any choice food by nightfall. He stared, his firm body looked shrunken and his black coat unwashed.

How do you explain to a cat his litter brother is dead?

As scrawny kittens, John and William suckled my roommate Vi's slippers side by side and played jungles among the houseplants. We taught them about the cat flap by sending their unwilling bodies through, paws askew. They sampled the exciting outside world together, oblivious of urban dangers.

And William paid the price of freedom under a car's wheels.

Vi thought another kitten, a William look-alike, might cheer John, but he was furious. The kitten stayed just one night, holed up in my room for safety, while John raged and hissed at Vi. Once a set of angry claws came under my door, scoring the wallpaper.

John gradually adapted to life after William, but more troubles followed. Without his ally, feral cats used the cat flap to invade, stealing John's food, battering his body, and spraying powerfully. We had a plague of fleas. Vi panicked openly whenever John was home late.

So the cat flap was blocked. John became an inside cat, sampling life at second-hand through glass, eyeing oblivious Glasgow pigeons. Happily, Vi's move to the country took place before John was too old to appreciate his private garden, with sweet earthy smells, grass under his paws, and all of life's delights accessible through his private cat flap.

No other cats by his wish. But perhaps William was around in spirit.

Each individual's grief is private and personal.

The Final Goodbye

by Patti Thompson

Puff was no longer my fluffy, fat feline. He was gaunt, wheezy, and sad. I knew the outcome of our visit to the vet, yet I clung to hope. When the final word came, I felt that Puff deserved my last measure of love to end his suffering. I cried all the way home with "Amazing Grace" playing on the radio, a fitting meditation for the last thing.

As is often the case, I tried to comfort myself by writing, but the words that came were not what I intended. I began writing

"A Shining Place" to the tune I had heard on the radio. It became my tribute to Puff for his twelve years of devotion. My husband wanted to include it in our book *Cat Hymns*, so we had to record the song for the compact disc. I cried during the session, as did the angelic voices who sang my words.

A friend asked if she could post the words on a Web site devoted to those who had experienced the loss of a pet. I agreed, and within the hour, she called me back to say that seventy-three people had responded. Each was so grateful for the comfort those words had brought them.

Encouraged by this, I wrote a play about "a shining place for cats to go when their nine lives are done." I still cry whenever I hear that song performed, but now they are tears of joy. A living memorial to Puff!

Nothing teaches the human heart so much as suffering; from it we must learn compassion and acceptance.

Love Lives Forever

by Gordon Forbes

A couple came to live nearby and brought their two cats with them. Tubbs was a British shorthair queen, about four years old. Her kitten went everywhere with her, and I got to know her because I had to go into many houses, take her out, and deliver her back home to her people. Later, she would learn to come home on her own; or when I was at work, Tubbs followed my parents back to the house after their walk. When the couple split up, the woman took the kitten and gave me Tubbs.

Tubbs seemed to be enormously happy on her own with us. After my father died, I looked after my mother for about three years and Tubbs kept her company, loving every minute of it. Eventually, my mother went into a nursing home and I was all by myself with my sweet, loving Tubbs. She seemed to be very happy with me for the next decade and lived to be sixteen and a half years old. The year before she died, Tubbs became blind, but she got used to it and felt her way about the house. Whenever she went outdoors, I went with her so she never got lost again. My sweet British queen died on Christmas Eve, 2001. I loved her very much and I still do, for love lives forever in the heart.

To love with all one's heart and one's whole being is the greatest human capacity.

Adopt Them or They Will Perish

by Theresa Mancuso

Through no fault of their own, literally thousands of kittens are born because cat owners permit their unneutered and unspayed felines to run free where they can find each other and breed generations of feral cats or shelter victims that will soon be put to sleep for want of homes. How can a civilized society be so immune to the horrific results of irresponsibility? And yet it happens all the time.

A recent visit to the shelter made me feel like crying, as I walked among the cages of pathetic but wonderful cats and dogs who looked hungrily into my face as if to say, *Will you be my mother?* True, you can't rescue them all. You can't take them all home, or soon you'd be unable to care for them financially, emotionally, and physically. You'd be overrun, too. But by adopting one or two cats and encouraging friends to do likewise, by standing firm about the necessity to spay and neuter pets, by refusing to buy from pet stores that support puppy and kitty mills, we can do our small part in trying to balance the outrageous deficiency in our society when it comes to pet responsibility. Yes, adopt them or they will perish. Do it soon.

We are the stewards of the earth. All that is ours to use on this planet must be guarded and preserved by prudence and care.

The Cat with Beautiful Eyes

by Fran Pennock Shaw

Meph had the coolest green eyes. He spoke through them. "I want tuna fish" or "Scratch my ears," his eyes would say, and we obeyed. Meph ruled and he knew it. This tuxedo tomcat was a benevolent ruler, though. He graciously shared his kingdom with us—my best friend and me. He allowed us to sit on his sofa bed, so long as we offered our laps and shoulders for his throne. He let us eat anything we wanted, so long as we gave him some. He let us come and go as we pleased, so long as he could do the same.

Meph was also a teacher. Still teenagers, struggling without parents to set the house rules, we learned responsibility when Meph adopted us. He taught us care and compassion and how to catch mice. He also showed us how to share the mice once they were caught.

As is often true with beloved mentors and beneficent rulers, Meph taught the most important of life's lessons with his passing. We don't know how old Meph was when he died, but I guess he was still in his prime, the victim, I know now, of living too fast, too free in a world too big. In the dangerous city, it was amazing he survived his roaming as long as he did. Us, too.

One day Meph didn't come home. We searched; we cried; we vowed to be more careful. But he never returned. I always picture his eyes saying, *Remember me with love.*

The eyes are the windows of the soul; they tell everything.

Falling for Brambles

by Paul Sutton

Have you ever just known you were meant to have a particular cat? One day while I was horseback riding through the woods, a kitten ran out of the bushes beside me. I gently picked it up and asked at the house nearby if they had lost a kitten. I learned that there had been a mother cat with two kittens but she had died, leaving them alone. A teacher from the local school managed to take one of them, but no one could catch the other, and here it was in my arms having run out to "find me." I asked the householder to keep him for me and collected him after my ride. This started a relationship with Brambles (named after the bushes he was found in) that was far too short.

Probably because he had his start in life outside, Brambles insisted on going outdoors. He simply would not be content contained in the house. And that was tragedy in the making. One day he came home with his tooth through his tongue, and the vet told me he must have been hit by a car. He wanted to cross the main road to get to the empty lots where there were plenty of mice to chase. Alas, one terrible, traumatic day, Brambles was struck by a car and died. The driver had taken him to the local vet, who identified Brambles by the photograph I brought in. Unfortunately, that's how roaming kitties all too often meet their end.

Even if you don't believe in destiny, it sometimes seems that certain things are meant to be. Go with the flow when your inner voice says yes.

When Kabootle Bit Me Goodbye

by Lauren L. Merryfield

Our beautiful fifteen-pound Himalayan, Kabootle, was only six and a half years old when he was diagnosed with irreversible renal failure. Kabootle's condition hit him suddenly and put me into near shock.

Kabootle was a loving, protective kitty, but sometimes a bit of a biter, too. His bite was often a sign of affection, but one day it became a sign of finality. He could not eat or drink much, and

I had been up all night helping him. I finally realized just how ill he was and kept telling him not to try so hard to please me, that he did not need my permission to call it quits. Around noon the next day, Kabootle played with his favorite toy, asked to be let out on the balcony although it was January, and then plopped himself into my lap. He was doing something quite ritualistic, and I knew what it meant—almost. He purred fervently, kneaded on me, rubbed his head against my hand, and then, chomp. He bit me. Now I knew that Kabootle was saying goodbye.

"No! No! Not my kitty!" I cried, unrelentingly heartbroken. But I realized that Kabootle expected me to help him go, so I called our mobile vet. The last time we saw him, Kabootle let each family member hold him and hear his purr for the last time. Then he dashed off and hid behind a chair. We said goodbye to his physical body, but his spirit remains with us always.

Letting go is the hardest part of loving another being.

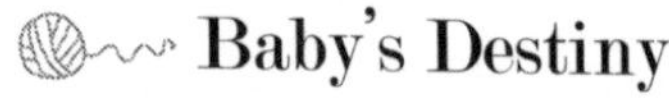

Baby's Destiny

by Sharon Ulrich

The Mae Bachur Animal Shelter opened its doors on a brisk early November morning, and by the end of the day, the kennels were overflowing with unwanted animals. Sadly, very few people visited the shelter over the following week, and the future of these animals looked grim. It was then that Baby entered our lives. She was the sole survivor of a litter of kittens that had been cannibalized by their mother, and we weren't even sure if she would survive the night. But from the start, she was a fighter. She quickly became the media darling. Her adorable tabby face appeared in both of the local newspapers, and her tiny mews even made a radio debut. Baby became a symbol of the fighting spirit of homeless animals everywhere, and the public couldn't get enough of her.

Then, on the eighteenth day of her life, Baby's trachea suddenly collapsed, and she died in my arms. It was a genetic defect, the veterinarian said; she never had a chance.

As I stood staring down at her lifeless body lying peacefully in my hands and tears streamed down my face, I suddenly realized what a huge gift Baby had given the community. She, like her siblings, wasn't meant to live. But her short life gave the shelter the public attention it needed, thereby saving the lives of the numerous cats and dogs that have since resided there. I think she always knew this was her destiny, and her soul can now rest in peace.

We cannot measure the quality of a life by length of time or material accomplishments.

Trixie

by Jackie S. Brooks

Our beautiful Trixie, the surrogate mother to a number of kittens over the years, was dying. Suddenly one day, she was not herself, and over the course of three weeks, she rapidly lost weight. It was summertime, and she wanted to be in the garden, lying under a shady bush. When she could no longer make it on her own, we carried her back and forth. We tried to tempt her with tiny morsels of chicken, but she could eat very little.

During this time, one of her "babies," who had gone missing eighteen months previously, suddenly reappeared. Tiggy appeared to have suffered a blow to the head and had partial memory loss. He wasn't sure of us, but he knew the house and he knew his mom.

For the three remaining weeks of Trixie's life, he followed her like a shadow and was always close by in the garden.

On Trixie's last morning, she lay in a corner of the living room, her paws moving back and forth as though she were dreaming of walking somewhere. I lay down on the floor beside her and started to gently stroke her side, speaking softly and quietly to her. I believe that God cares for all His creatures and that He has a special place for them, too, so I told her to walk into the light. A short time later, she passed away quietly.

We mourned the passing of a beautiful personality and hope one day to be reunited with her.

The bond we share with our mothers is mystical as well as physical.

No More Cats . . . Or So I Thought

by Dana Smith-Mansell

I lost Pete (eighteen) and Jace (fourteen) within a few years of each other. They had become my pets when I was a young teenager, and grew with me into adulthood. When they passed, I vowed I wouldn't get another cat. It just hurt too much to lose them! A few days after I buried Pete, I packed up the "cat belongings" and transported them to the local shelter. In my heart of hearts, I knew my "cat days" were over.

I arrived at the shelter, arms loaded with kitty treasures. I entered the cat room to sign the donation book. As I struggled to not look around, my eyes betrayed me and fell upon a black kitten. I tried in earnest to look away, but I couldn't. This kitty was calling to me. The workers (very observant) saw my interest, and insisted I visit her. I complied, *knowing* I was not leaving with a cat. As I entered the cage, this kitten leaped and landed gracefully on my shoulder, her purrs resonating in my ear. Tears came to my eyes as the staff related the story of her rescue, along with her mother, from a drainpipe in which they had been stuck. Another kitten had died. Needless to say, I went to the store to purchase new cat supplies.

Kearsey is fourteen years old, lives with a permanent limp, and sounds like a truck rolling across the floor, but her infirmity never impedes her life. She has shown us that anything is possible!

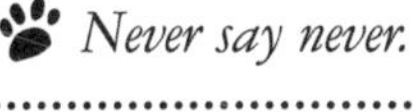

Never say never.

Ginger's Tragedy

by Elli Matlin

My cat Ginger was half-Persian and half–Maine coon, back in the times when Maine coon cats had a bounty on them in the state of Connecticut. My family owned a summer place in North Franklin, Connecticut, and next door there was a working dairy farm. The farmer had a Persian cat that got out, and by the end of the summer there were kittens. The farmer told us that the kittens were about six weeks old and were eating solid food, but when we got home with the kitten he gave us, it was obvious that she was younger and still nursing.

My mother took a bottle from one of my dolls, punctured a hole in the nipple, and hand-raised this tiny kitten. Ginger was carried around in my mother's apron pocket (you can see how long ago this was—my mother wore an apron!) all day long. Ginger grew into a big beautiful tortoiseshell cat that weighed about seventeen pounds, and she lived a good life, but unfortunately died from smoke inhalation in a house fire. That was a tragedy for our whole family. After the fire, we found Ginger curled up on my brother's electric train table, without so much as a singed hair.

Tragedy touches every life in some degree. The best way to prepare for such dark moments is to cultivate a deliberate faith in life and a sense of hope.

....

Old Salt

by Rod Marsden

Since before Lord Nelson could tie his own shoelaces, there have been cats aboard fighting vessels. There was a time when no British ship's crew would go easily out to sea without their favorite feline. The tradition was not lost on the Aussies. When I sailed with the Royal Australian Navy as a peacetime observer, I met a cat named Old Salt.

Old Salt was a scruffy-looking mongrel ginger. He had a sleek body, despite getting tidbits from everybody on the ship.

Taken aback when a bunch of amateurs came aboard, he winced as we bumped into overhead beams and tripped over fire hoses. He meowed when someone stepped in his water bowl, and was most indignant when anyone failed to look to see if a chair was occupied. Still, like the rest of the regular crew, Old Salt persevered with us until we were shipshape, with no hard feelings about earlier episodes. We were only human, and cats do believe in giving humans a second chance.

Since then, Old Salt has passed away and was buried at sea, which is only fitting and proper. He has probably joined the deceased cats of fighting vessels and is riding on the seas of heaven in a ship built for such felines. There are probably humans aboard doing what humans do. Perhaps cats can't imagine a heaven without humans, just like we can't imagine a world without cats.

Bearers of tradition play an important role in keeping us all aware of our place in history.

Katzenberg's Journey to Rainbow Bridge

by Diane Bell (a.k.a. Diabella)

6:00 P.M.: I lose the dearest cat I ever had. A thousand stars fell and the moon cried.

6:15 P.M.: The angels read the Book of Judgment and take Katzenberg to heaven.

9:00 P.M.: He is awarded the Good Cat Medal of Honor. He thanks the Keeper of Heaven's Gate but says that he is tired and needs to go home to his family.

11:15 P.M.: He finds the staircase that brought him to heaven and asks for directions to get home. "No," says the Bubble Fairy, "You are going to a place far beyond the stars. A place they call Rainbow Bridge." Frightened and exhausted, he falls asleep on the stairway.

The Sun Fairy announces a new day and all things beautiful awaken. The Good Fairy Aurora appears. She speaks of the wonders of the Bridge, promises Katzenberg that a surprise meeting will take place, and helps him cross over. Minutes later the surprise comes to pass, for out of nowhere Katzenberg's old buddy Handsome appears. Suddenly realizing that he left his medal in heaven, he asks a bluebird to carry a message to the Good Fairy Aurora. Within moments the medal falls from the heavens into his paws, upon which he presents it to Handsome.

Until we meet again, my funny valentine, I bid you farewell. There will never be another as generous of spirit or as loving as you were. May you find many mice and many pleasures across the Bridge. You've earned them.

Like bread cast upon the water, Holy Scripture says, our good deeds return to us a hundredfold.

....

Previously published on Diane Bell's Web site (*http://diabellalovescats.com/trop.htm*) and condensed for this book.

The Afterlife

by Lillian Howell

When I was eight, I saw a friend's kittens and I wanted one, but since they were all spoken for, I was told we couldn't have one. I wouldn't give up. I knew that our family previously owned a cat to catch mice because we lived on a farm. Every Christmas and birthday I would ask for a kitten. Eventually, my parents gave in and we got a lovely tabby kitten that became a favorite of the family as well as a good mouser. The people who gave us the kitten thought it was female and so we named her Queenie.

When the vet told us our kitten was male, it was already too late to change his name. He had to live with Queenie. Queenie loved to sit on top of a single fencepost at the back of the house. He stayed there for hours, and we couldn't figure out why.

One day, sadly, my father found his body on the road about half a mile away, near some houses. It was too late to do anything for Queenie, so he took the body home and told my mother what had happened. We gave Queenie a peaceful resting place in the garden.

When Queenie came walking back into the yard from the dead, a few days later, father was astonished. Queenie lived for many years after that, and we never found out whose cat was buried in our garden.

Life is a precious gift that must not be squandered.

Those Four Most Dreaded Words

by Lauren L. Merryfield

When our feline members of the family die, not only do we experience a terrible grief, we also discover an unwelcome reaction from others—the dreaded, "It's only a cat!"

In my work as a cofacilitator in a pet-loss support group, this lack of empathy from others was often expressed as one of the hardest aspects of the grieving process. Some felt guilt in the extreme nature of their grief, as if their whole world had crumbled now that their beloved cat was gone. This sadness is often coupled with feelings of guilt when the grieving person has made the decision of euthanasia.

"I had no idea it would hit me so hard," they weep. "And I feel even worse when someone says 'it' was only a cat."

A safe place to grieve is as important during the loss of a cat as with the loss of a human. People need to be given the space and the permission to feel their sadness, with all of its strange twists and turns.

Grief is a universal experience expressed individually by each of us. To respect and be compassionate of the grief of another is a basic responsibility.

Elmo and Zoey

by Karen Lanman

It is said that each ending is a new beginning. Our ending was the passing of our two-year-old daughter from leukemia. The beginning was the wonderful spirits that entered our lives the very afternoon of the funeral. My husband, Mark, and I decided to get a pet to be my companion at home, especially while Mark was working nights.

We set out to find our feline soul mate that same Saturday. It had been raining off and on all day, but as the hot Texas afternoon wore on, the sky darkened by the second. We went to several shelters, but strangely enough, the outcomes were not good. Either we were too late (closed), or there were no kittens available for adoption.

As we made our last stop of the day, the sun peeked through the clouds. We opened the door and walked in; there, in a small wire cage, were two Siamese kittens (a brother and sister). I fell in love immediately. My husband said, "Either we take them both home, or we keep looking." I answered without hesitation, "Both." After buying half of the cat aisle at the local pet store, we set out for home.

Our kittens grew into wonderful members of the family. Elmo and Zoey possess some characteristics so similar to our daughter that people have to see them to believe it. We couldn't imagine life without them and their constant unconditional love. We are thankful for them each and every day.

Animals are often healers of human suffering, especially the pain of loss.

Conclusion

Blessed are those who have experienced the utter delight of knowing and loving wonderful companion cats. There is nothing quite like the presence of a cat in the house to make you feel at home, whether it's a mansion or the tiniest inner city apartment, a rustic cabin or royal palace. Cats are like a little bit of heaven on earth, their purring not unlike the stir of angel wings. An unknown person said, "Dogs believe they are human. Cats believe they are God."

For me, cats lend a charm and sweetness to life, and what they demand in return is minimal by comparison. When I was a child, I longed for a cat but had not, so when required at school to memorize poems about cats, I did so with relish. I still remember some of them by heart. Indeed, our feline friends watch over us as they sit on their silent haunches, perched here and there in our homes. But they do not move on. They stay with us forever, not only in the memories we cherish, but in every good quality we acquire by knowing them through the years and living better because of it.

Contributors

Margaret Ambler has always been fascinated with cats and has wanted to help as many as possible. Margaret, thirty-eight, lives out in the countryside, and has been involved in feline rescue for many years.

Camilla Baird has been breeding Korats for ten years, and is the only Korat breeder in Denmark. Camilla shares her life with her husband and his Russian Blues.

Dory Bartell is blind. In addition to one active Labrador service dog and one retired Lab, Dory has several cats. She considers animals the best therapy anyone could ask for.

Diane Bell (a.k.a. Diabella) shares her home in New York with Dracula, Red-Devil, Witch-Hazel, and Tropicana, and is known on the Web as "Diabella" for her cat rescue/fantasy/graphics site. You can visit her at *www.diabellalovescats.com*.

Jose Antonio Brito, born in the Dominican Republic, came to the United States at the age of ten, and speaks three languages fluently: Spanish, English, and Portuguese. Jose is employed by the New York City Department of Probation.

Jackie S. Brooks lives in North Yorkshire, UK. Her work has been published on *Clevermag.com* and also in the local newspaper. Several of Jackie's poems are to be published in different anthologies this year.

Mercedes M. Cardona is a journalist in New York. Born in San Juan, Puerto Rico, she has worked as a newspaper and magazine writer and editor since graduating from George Washington University in 1984. She lives with her cat, Ms. Kitty, in Forest Hills, New York.

Patricia Clements, BA, MA, is researching material from ex–Far East Prisoners of War for her PhD thesis. She runs an animal sanctuary for the old, sick, and terminally ill in Wales, UK. Pat is author of *Working with Children, Sticky Dewi,* and *A Cat in Every Corner.* She is also a columnist for *Cat World* magazine and teaches art in her spare time.

Brenda Colbourne lives in Canberra, Australia, with her more-than-thirty rescue cats.

Paulette Cooper is the author of fifteen books, including the award-winning *277 Secrets Your Cat Wants You to Know* (Ten Speed Press) and *277 Secrets Your Dog Wants You to Know* (Ten Speed Press). Over the years, Paulette has been owned by five cats and six dogs.

Barbara Custer is a respiratory therapist who has been writing horror and science-fiction stories for about eight years. Her work appears in small press magazines such as *Fading Shadows*, *The Ultimate Unknown*, and *Masque Noir*. She recently published a novel, *Twilight Healer*, through First Books Library. Barbara lives in Pennsylvania with her husband Michael.

Peter P. Dachille, Jr. is a freelance photographer (his cat Sam is a frequent and willing subject), a sometime writer, a volunteer painter (walls, not canvases), and a full-time program assistant in a college literacy department. He is a lifelong Brooklynite.

Toni Eames, MS, **and Ed Eames,** PhD, adjunct professors of sociology at California State University, Fresno, live with their Golden Retriever guide dogs, Escort and Latrell; a retired guide dog, Echo; and cats, Bonanza, Kismet, Cali, and Nifty. They have published two books and write for many animal and disability-related magazines. Both are recipients of prestigious Maxwell Awards from the Dog Writers Association of America.

Rebecca Eitemiller is twelve years old. She calls herself "a total cat freak." Becky lives in Salkum, Washington, with her mom, their three dogs, and two cats, Sassy and Snickers. Becky attends Onalaska Middle School, where she is currently in the sixth grade.

Audrey Elias lives in Brooklyn, New York. When she lived alone, the neighborhood strays passed the word that she was a soft touch, and at one point Audrey had nine rescue cats. Then she acquired a dog, a husband, and three children, and the strays stopped coming around.

Susan M. Ewing writes a weekly column, "The Pet Pen," for the *Post-Journal* of Jamestown, New York. She is the author of *The Pembroke Welsh Corgi: Family Friend and Farmhand.* Susan is treasurer of the Cat Writers' Association. She lives in Jamestown, New York, with her husband, Jim, and their three Corgis.

Anne Fawcett studies veterinary science at the University of Sydney. She lives with several former patients (Mike and Lil, short for Lil' Puss) and her husband, Jamie.

Gordon Forbes lives in Dumfries, Scotland. As a photographer, Gordon has won 200 photography awards. (The world record is 250.)

Pam Fuoco is a retired claims adjuster and unit manager for the former Travelers Insurance Company. She lives in upstate New York. Pam has a million interests that include Marilyn, the family cat.

P. M. Griffin is the author of fifteen novels, including two brand-new Star Commandos books and nine short stories in the challenging realms of science fiction and fantasy. Her two Cat Writers' Association Muse Medallion Awards attest to her love of and commitment to cats. She lives in Brooklyn, New York.

Anna Haltrecht lives on Salt Spring Island, British Columbia, with two feline brothers, Bamboo and Snowball, her partner, Ian, and his son, Dustin, and Daisy the Dog.

Karen Heist was born in Columbus, Ohio, and grew up in south New Jersey. She lives in Holland, Pennsylvania, with four cats and a dog.

Tracy Heyman, a part-time freelance writer and full-time Web site designer, is a frequent contributor to cat magazines and a member of the Cat Writers' Association (CWA) and the Society of Children's Book Writers and Illustrators (SCBWI). Tracy lives in Baltimore, Maryland, where she is completing her master's degree in creative writing.

Linnette Horne lives in Wellington, New Zealand. Cats have been in her family for as long as she can remember. She has had nonfiction articles published in New Zealand.

John Hosp and his wife Michelle live in Salt Lake City, Utah, where John is an assistant professor in the Department of Special Education at the University of Utah. He is Rose Hosp's son.

Rose Hosp resides with her husband in rural central New York. She is a retired high school teacher, now teaching part-time at Utica College.

Lillian Howell, a fourth-generation cat lover, on the female line, of course, is a freelance writer. She is married and has an eleven-year-old daughter. The Howells have three cats.

Tina Juul has owned Maine Coon cats all her life, but she greatly appreciates the virtues of mixed breeds. Tina lives in Denmark with her giant Maine coon and her little one-time stray. She works in the travel industry.

Ed Kostro is a freelance writer and member of the Cat Writers' Association. His work has appeared in *Catholic Digest*, *ByLine Magazine*, *The Almanac for Farmers & City Folk*, *Pets: Part of the Family*, *PetLife*, *and*

Cats. His new book, called *Curious Creatures—Wondrous Waifs, My Life with Animals*, depicts his fifty-year love affair with animals, and has just been published. He resides in Illinois with his wife Rebecca, five felines, and two rambunctious canines.

Karen Lanman lives in Allen, Texas.

Angela London works as a naturopathic physician in the Pacific Northwest, where she lives with her two-year-old daughter, Olivia Carolina.

Daphne R. Macpherson is a CSR for a nationwide insurance company. She breeds and shows Balinese and Siamese cats from British Columbia to Oregon, specializing in red points.

Louise Maguire can't pass a cat without speaking to it and better still stroking its fur. The cat's gentle purring response at ankle level delights Louise, but not her jealous dog.

Edy Makariw grew up in the suburbs in a two-parent, three-child, and four-cat household. No stranger to bringing in strays, she now fosters for a local rescue group.

Rod Marsden's short stories have been published in Australia, England, Russia, and the United States. His first novel, *20th Century Dart*, is now available through the Web site *www.1stbooks.com*. Rod lives on the south coast of New South Wales, Australia.

Elli Matlin always has a couple of rescued cats living comfortably in her home. A veritable walking encyclopedia of animal care, Elli was an art teacher in the public schools until her retirement several years ago. Elli recently moved from Brooklyn to Rock Hill, New York.

Lyn McConchie owns a small farm where she raises colored sheep and shares her nineteenth-century farmhouse with 7,000 books and two

Ocicats, Tiger and Dancer. Her writing has appeared in the United States, Canada, the UK, Poland, Russia, Australia, and New Zealand.

Kimberly McDowell is an animal rights activist who has fostered and cared for numerous feral cat families. She has four inside cats that were all rescued from shelters or rescue centers.

Caroline McRae-Madigan lived the first fifteen years of her life in a tiny Canadian town called Burks Falls, Ontario (population 900). Since then she has traveled all across Canada and settled down in Blind River, Ontario, another tiny town.

Lauren L. Merryfield is the editor/publisher of Catlines at *www.catliness.com*. Lauren and her husband Jim have three cats, Jasper, Mikey, and Gabrielle. She has been published in several Kernel Books, *Heartwarmers of Love* and *God's Messengers*. Lauren is a member of the Cat Writers' Association, the Association for Pet Loss and Bereavement, and the Cat Collector's Organization.

Catherine Miller is a mental health professional who lives among the redwood trees in northern Californian wine country. She journeyed westward from New York to California in 1986 and has never looked back. Her short fiction for children and adults has appeared in *The Storyteller*, *Kids' Highway*, *Skipping Stones*, *Short Stories Bimonthly*, *Phoebe*, and other journals.

Glenda Moore lives and works in Utah as a computer assistant. She shares her house with ten cats and a husband. Glenda's published work includes an article in Franklin Dohanyos's book *The Cats of Our Lives: Funny and Heartwarming Reminiscences of Feline Companions.* Visit "Cat Stuff" at *www.xmission.com/~emailbox*.

Fran Nickerson, a retired Tonkinese breeder, has shared her home with Tonkinese cats since 1964. Fran's cats are behind the pedigrees of most Tonkinese in this country. Her cat "descendants" are in Japan, Australia, and South Africa.

Carol Osborne lives on top of a mountain in Floyd County, Virginia, on the Blue Ridge Parkway. She has been raising cats for about thirty years.

Maxine Perchuk grew up in Brooklyn and makes her home there with her cats, Sylvester and Isadora, and her dogs, Willie and Beatrice. She is a New York City Probation Officer assigned to Family Court. Maxine is currently earning her master's degree in school psychology.

Yvette Piantadosi resides in North Carolina with her husband Mike and five children. Yvette has bred and raised German shepherds and Malinois for many years, but Dinky the cat owns her and her family and considers himself overseer of all newborn pups.

Pat Ramirez lives in northern Virginia and works as a legal secretary. Her spare time is devoted to volunteer work and Siamese rescue.

Donna M. Ramsay, a lifelong animal lover, resides in Arizona, knowing that animals bring great joy and wonders to all that choose to enrich their lives with the presence of these wonderful creatures.

Mary Rodgers Easton was born in Guanajuato, Mexico, and now makes her home in Grand Prairie, Texas. She is retired from teaching school and makes her home with four much loved cats.

Lisa Sanders is twenty-one years old and lives in Monroe, North Carolina, where she works as a photo lab supervisor for CVS pharmacy.

Fran Pennock Shaw, who lives in Lancaster, Pennsylvania, is president of the international Cat Writers' Association, Inc. She has published nearly 200 companion animal articles in newspapers and magazines and has been honored many times by CWA, Dog Writers' Association of America, the Pennsylvania Veterinary Medical Association, and various journalism organizations. She was a contributing writer to *Symptom Solver for Dogs and Cats* published by Rodale Press in 1999.

Mary Shen lives on the Lower East Side of New York City. She participates in and often leads exercise classes for seniors, and enjoys occasional trips, having recently visited the Great Wall of China and the markets in Hong Kong.

Gail Smart lived in the London suburbs all of her life, but now, retired, Gail's home is in Kent with her dogs, cats, and several rescued feral cats that use the stables where her horses used to be kept.

Dana Smith-Mansell resides in the "coal regions" of Pennsylvania with her husband, cat, and "terrier trio." New Horizon Press published her children's book, *Stop Bullying Bobby!*, in 2004.

Diana "Sue" Snyder is a single mom of a six-year-old son. They live in a small, rural town in northwestern Louisiana. Diana breeds Bengal kittens and is currently designing new cat furniture.

Miriam Stewart has lived in New York State all of her life and has always had a cat, except for the past three years. She is married and has two sons and five grandchildren.

Paul Sutton is a fifty-five-year-old woman with a man's name. She lives in Kent, England, with her sister, her horse, three cats, and her three adored Collies, Whisper, Summer, and Sunny.

Patti Thompson lives in Tupelo, Mississippi, with her husband, Stephen, and her cats, Miss Kritter, Scar, Peaches, and Mouse. She co-wrote the book *Cat Hymns* (Quail Ridge Press, 1997) and two plays based on the *Cat Hymns* characters.

Sharon Ulrich is a feline behaviorist and resident cat expert for Humane Society Yukon. Sharon currently resides in Whitehorse, Yukon, with her husband, two children, four cats, and two dogs.

Barbara H. Vinson was born and raised in Indianapolis, Indiana. Barbara lived and worked in New York City in the medical milieu for many years, but recently retired and relocated her cats and household to northeastern Minnesota, at the edge of the Boundary Waters Canoe Area Wilderness.

John R. "Jack" Vinson (1940–2004), seemed to never stop working, even after retirement. His cats and dogs were truly his best friends.

Selma L. Wiener was born and raised in the Bronx. Although an only child, there was always a pet cat in her life. After retiring from her teaching career as a biology instructor, Selma settled down to a happy new life with her pet cat, Missy.

Lorraine Williams lives in New Zealand, where she is a published writer of children's stories, articles, plays, and adult short fiction.

Kari Winters is a Board-Certified Advanced Practice Registered Nurse and also a member of the Cat Writers' Association. She contributes frequently to *The Pet Press* in Los Angeles, as well as humane organization newsletters, and has won many awards for her writing. She is the author of the book *Princess Fiona: My Purrsonal Story*.

Autumn sie Wolf is a Michigander living in Indiana with her husband, horses, cats, dogs, cavies, goats, ferrets, and birds. She is a mother, zookeeper, artist, teacher, veteran, and screen printer.

About the Author

Theresa Mancuso, a writer, photographer, and graphic designer, has always loved animals. She has lived with German shepherd dogs and numerous cats for more than twenty years and credits them with helping her achieve great contentment in her creative work. Theresa's animals have inspired several books, dozens of articles, and thousands of photographs.

By creating animal-themed T-shirts for kids in her neighborhood, distributed at will, Theresa spreads the good news of interspecies communication and devotion. The covers of her books are available on T-shirts, thanks to her generous publisher, Adams Media. Theresa also designs custom T-shirts for those who want their own cats' photos to be used.

You can contact Theresa Mancuso by e-mail at:
geisty@verizon.net.